Soul Talk,
Song Language

Soul Talk, Song Language

Conversations with Joy Harjo

Joy Harjo and Tanaya Winder

Photographs by Joy Harjo

WESLEYAN UNIVERSITY PRESS
MIDDLETOWN, CONNECTICUT

Wesleyan University Press
Middletown CT 06459
www.wesleyan.edu/wespress
© 2011 Joy Harjo and Tanaya Winder
All rights reserved
Manufactured in the United States of America
Designed by Katherine B. Kimball
Typeset in Sabon by Alice W. Bennett
5 4 3 2 1
Wesleyan University Press is a member of the Green Press Initiative.
The paper used in this book meets their minimum requirement
for recycled paper.

Library of Congress Cataloging-in-Publication Data
Harjo, Joy.
Soul talk, song language : conversations with Joy Harjo / Joy
Harjo and Tanaya Winder ; photographs by Joy Harjo.
p. cm.
ISBN 978-0-8195-7150-2 (cloth : alk. paper) —
ISBN 978-0-8195-7151-9 (e-book)
1. Harjo, Joy—Interviews. 2. Indian authors—Interviews.
3. Indians in literature. 4. Indians of North America—Ethnic identity.
I. Winder, Tanaya. II. Title.
PS3558.A62423Z46 2011
811'.54—dc22   2011021768

FRONTISPIECE: "Earth Breathing." © Joy Harjo .

Contents

II. Columns by Joy Harjo

Foreword

A Carrier of Memory

In this volume of interviews and collected writings, Joy Harjo acts as a guide, taking us on a journey into her identity as a woman and as an artist, poised between poetry and music, encompassing tribal heritage, productive reassessments, and comparisons with the American cultural patrimony. But even before presenting herself in an exquisitely literary context, she proudly underlines her Indian roots, and this all-embracing assertion unceasingly leaves a profoundly coherent mark on form and content. Thus these interviews accompany the reader on a human and professional itinerary, where the reading of her poems is often an illuminating exegetic commentary, directly or more often perceptibly, but at the same time it speaks of the place and time where her inspiration was born.

From the very beginning, it communicates a cultural background that draws on family habits—painting and music—the former from her grandmother Naomi Harjo and her great-aunt Lois Harjo ("I found a great refuge in the act of drawing"), the latter from her mother ("my mother was a singer, so we had music and her voice often holding our home together"), up to the moment of her escape from Oklahoma to New Mexico to study at the Institute of American Indian Arts (IAIA), and subsequently at the University of Iowa. Her initial relationship with this university was problematic, due to the quality of its teaching ("too male and white oriented") and the gap between her educational background and that of other students, in an environment where the artistic sensibility included nothing of her tribal tradition ("I felt a stranger there"). But the strength of her inner world, her great creative inspiration, although "married with great despair" as a result of a painful sense of discomfort and harsh everyday difficulties, nevertheless projected her toward increasing acquirement of her means of expression. Her success as a poet, after a relatively short period of writing, is displayed in numerous volumes. Her work is attracting a growing readership, and has drawn the attention of critics in the United States and elsewhere, as well as in several university courses dedicated to her production, giving rise to high-quality degree dissertations.

In this collection of interviews there unfolds a detailed discussion of the complex material from which she derives her inspiration, a testimony that points to a relentless drive toward the truth in the many worlds that she passes through, always animated by the desire to find an area of light, sometimes in a harsh clash with reality. But the first thing to emerge from her writer's laboratory is the close anchoring of her poetry to orality, with the result that "written text is, for me, fixed orality": it thus goes back to a performance she remembers and it transmits an oral act, in which the moment of speaking and listening unites the poet and her audience in a single inseparable unit. Hence the creation of a mixed genre, or cross-genre writing, is increasingly present in her more recent works. These are compositions from which several voices emerge—poems, prose poems, stories, commentaries preceding the poems, which are generally created "to mimic oral presentations," or as a reflection of an oral experience of poetry. In the answers that Harjo gives, this concept is often repeated, and from this, in turn, there emerges music as a natural continuity, not so much as a bridge between two genres, but because "the roots of poetry lead to music." Since poetry is a sound art, as she affirms, music, singing voice, and spoken poetic word converge together "as one voice."

Music, and in particular that of the saxophone, to which she has turned her hand in recent years, is often mentioned in these interviews. Besides speaking of a beloved Indian ancestor who played the same instrument, of her band, or of individual musicians like Larry Mitchell, with whom she often performs, she specifies that by so doing, she creates a performance in which she challenges the current way of interpreting the utilization of poetry: indeed "That was the original impetus of the poetry, and of the sax, to find a way to sing: I still want my poems to stand up on their own. This will make me even more a maverick in the poetry world, in this country at least. I don't enjoy academic reverie."

Thus Harjo's work now includes aspects different from those that it displayed initially: the written word also becomes a voice modulated with traditional tones—songs and chants, which radiate a music that springs from her saxophone. But the sonorities that come into being are not an accompaniment or a musical tempo, but rather intimate unions of words, voices, and sounds which convey the blend and interpenetration of meanings and rhythms, perfectly harmonized in a continual reciprocal reflection. A performance like this goes beyond its own communicative act, and becomes the expression of a culture, as she says, captured in its deepest roots, and modulated with a sense of belonging and continuity. The contribution of modern sonorities such as blues is suggestive not so much of influences, but of a revitalization of a kind of music born and cultivated in the tribal environment. This is the awareness that animates the poetics and musical activity of Joy Harjo, intent as she is on not leaving any empty spaces between words, voice, and music.

The answers to the various interviewers depict a world in which the things of life emerge and are transmitted by an energy that unites people, plants, and animals, "an engagement and not a dominant concept" but something "that opens everything up." Her poetic expression, thus interpreted, allows her "to speak directly in a language that was intended to destroy us" or, to quote another famous text of hers on Native American women writers, edited with Gloria Bird, "reinventing the enemy's language." It is a language at the basis of so-called "minority literature"—Indian, in this case—a label that Harjo identifies as a "power trick" because, she affirms, the geographic expanse of tribal cultures covers an immense extension from one end of the globe to the other, including major literary traditions: "It's the fearful ones who try and keep us out who are still looking for a place." And she goes on: "This 'American culture' is young and rootless. It is adolescent with an adolescent sense of time and place, that is 'here and now,' with no reference or power rooted in the earth, ancestors, or historical and mythical sense. Value your community and what that has to offer, and continue to reach out beyond what you know, and grow fresh ideas, meetings between borders, new roots."

This continual aspiration to an inner growth, the need for a dialogue with the multiple heritage of the past, with everything that moves around human beings, in the contrast that arises with contemporary America, is summed up in another highly perceptive affirmation regarding the mainstream culture of the United States:

> I have always called the U.S. culture the "over-culture" and don't consider it a true culture. Belief, social institutions, art, and traditions construct culture. The United States is made up of many cultures. There is no such thing as a melting pot. There are various cultural streams that are renewed, slowed, cut off, or otherwise changed. The over-culture is a culture of buying and selling.

Furthermore, this bitter appraisal pervades her awareness of tragic events in contemporary America, besieged by violence and imperialistic forays which in the end provoke further violence at the heart of its own territory: its onset may appear to be sudden, "but there is a trail that goes back, like roots." And these are the same roots that go back to the distant past, that is to say, almost as far back as the ethnocide of the tribal peoples. This is a reflection that brings with it the landscape of the American West, full of history and wounds, and at the same time remembered and celebrated as an "intimate connection," lands which have nourished a never-ending journey, together with the landscape of Hawai'i, where Harjo lived for many years, "to learn water"; "when water is the prevailing influence everything in the atmosphere carried its essence of being."

The representation of Harjo's activity extends to the role and the responsibility of artists: they must bring a testimony of experience in the present, but also a renewal in the wake of tradition; they promote and regenerate art and culture, sometimes communicating with their public almost beyond the realm of words, if the communicative act takes place in perfect reciprocal integrity, if words are used to usher in transformation. In this context, then, to write poetry "is to move into the world and effect change," and that includes artists and their public, both part of the poem.

Starting from these premises, Joy Harjo describes why she wrote two children's books (*The Good Luck Cat* and *For a Girl Becoming*), not just to mark the birth of her grandchildren, but above all to cement relationships and responsibilities, to inspire an intimately reciprocal sense, to make sure that "all children are able to see themselves in each other," "to re-imagine themselves as beautiful and powerful . . . moved to dream and share." All this derives from considering that her generation was taught to read by the Dick and Jane series, in which, rather than being created for children, the stories described an orderly, aseptic social reality, closed to everything that was not a part of the mainstream way of life, the same primer so perspicaciously described and progressively altered by Toni Morrison in *The Bluest Eye*.

Although different in its aims and functions, Joy Harjo's teaching experience—she has several times held courses of creative writing at prestigious universities—is based on the same principles: "Study with all parts of your being, not just your intellect. Some of your knowledge may come from books, most of it from other sources." Such teaching transcends the formal techniques, always leading to an interrelation of all things, from which knowledge and true understanding are born. Bearing in mind the frequently mentioned sense of reciprocity, this teaching experience "can feed the writing," "unless you are involved in academic politics and fights."

On other battles, Joy Harjo as a woman does not fail to speak her mind, expressing appreciation for the achievements of feminism, which has undoubtedly inspired significant changes, though many of these aspirations do not accord with the organization of the tribal world. However, in our modern-day world, she adds, we are still surrounded by a system in which everything connected with female experience is underestimated. Starting from its conception of the world, Christianity cancels every female presence, whereas there can be no creative power without any female force.

In her articles for the *Muscogee Nation News*, she almost always starts by watching what is happening in the natural world. This view, with its inner harmony, clashes with what she sees in our society: stereotyped images of Indians, identity issues, fabricated or false stories giving rise to festivities like Thanksgiving, Hollywood movies about Native tribes, or the dehumanized way of living in a society where massacres and racism are the inexorable outcomes. Harjo's thoughts turn instead to global roots and ancient trades by which almost everything traveled all over the world, connecting peoples and cultures. The same can be said for our creation of our own stories, which means that we pass on family, clan, and tribal knowledge from one generation to another, making time and space larger than we can imagine.

In the six pieces with which the volume closes the poet merges with the witness, not only of her times, but also of the past, conserving a moral and historical legacy engraved in her memory. The common denominator is an act of resistance as a safeguard against the wounds inflicted on the earth, to defend what a person is—although considered in various ways inferior because he or she does not fit neatly into the mold of civilization. By the same token, then, the term 'act of resistance' can also be used for the work of Patricia Grace, who was celebrated by Harjo when she was awarded the Neustadt International Prize for Literature. Grace is considered to be an ambassador for Maori writing and culture; her stories mingle her tradition with Western forms of contemporary literature. This is a way for all tribal cultures to remain anchored to the past, while renewing their tradition.

And lastly there is the critic who skillfully enters into the intimate communicative process of epistolary literature in her afterword for *The Delicacy and Strength of Lace*, with the same "delicacy" that can be found in this exchange of letters between James Wright and Leslie Marmon Silko. Harjo detects, in the words of both, all the painful implications, or the peaceful flow of ordinary daily life, marked by sounds and colors that softly illuminate moments that may appear to be common, but which enclose inside them the savor of deep knowledge and the tranquil beauty of everything that surrounds us. It is a union of poetry and storytelling, says Harjo, and of human and literary voices which meet and share this interlaced pattern. Harjo, an artist herself, enters into this kind of creative laboratory, recognizing "the struggle to be artists in the midst of the daily challenges of living."

But being a poet is also a challenge that expands, in order to reconstruct this land called America. With the strength of writing, of poetry, of myths, it is possible to lay the foundations for a change, and to penetrate with language a spiral of cognitive experience, the essence that genuinely gives meaning to the life of our intellect and our spirit. This is a concept of poetic art where there is no place for higher forms of poetry that descend from the European tradition, as has already been repeated in various interviews. Beyond every hierarchy of value, poetry interprets and consigns to us the world to which we belong, always looking for vision, as when Harjo goes out in search of a glimpse of sky early in the morning, above the neon totem poles in Times Square, to present her four-day-old fourth granddaughter to the sun: the affirmation of a harmonious relationship, the celebration of a sacred commission that gives certainty to our life. Like the sun, above the rain in New York. Like poetry. "The Last Word."

What emerges as a distinctive characteristic from this wide-ranging, insightful series of interviews is a constant boundary-crossing: varieties of genres, which are however linked together in a precise cognitive itinerary; the blending of the oral and the written to inform each other; the poetic sound of words and the sound of the sax; the woman and the artist telling of a perfect osmosis between life and writing; the water of Hawai'i and the New Mexico desert; a pervasive call-and-response that Harjo always seeks from her audience. In these detailed responses, Harjo weaves a tapestry where every strand evokes a further pattern. It's a dynamic process which continually opens up new possibilities of knowledge and artistic experimentation. And it is the testimony of a generous, fully convinced commitment which brings the past and the culture of her people to life with all the incisive mastery of modern means of expression, yet constantly draws on the strength of a memory, experienced not as an inert instrument, but as a driving power in the definition of an identity and in its affirmation in contemporary America.

Joy Harjo lives in many different worlds, and by means of these interviews, she not only allows us to enter into her creative laboratory but she also draws a moving geography of the soul, a sort of irregular autobiography that possesses an extraordinary narrative effectiveness. The reader perceives that she is always intensely dedicated to reaching, or recovering, intangible perfections or visions in her search as a woman and an artist.

Laura Coltelli is a professor of American literature at the University of Pisa, Italy. Her publications include *Winged Words: American Indian Writers Speak* (1990) and an edited collection of essays, *Reading Leslie Marmon Silko*.

Acknowledgments

My gratitude with singing and some saxophone riffs to Suzanna Tamminen for her enthusiasm and belief in this project; to Stephanie Elliot for her support and encouragement; to LeAnne Fields for urging the project on; *mvto* to Becca Landsberry, Ruth Bible, and the rest of the *Muscogee Nation News* staff for their assistance; to Laura Coltelli for discernment, friendship, and the impeccable introduction; to Tanaya Winder for her assistance, precise words and thoughts; and—for my poetry, writing, and music ancestors and descendants—*mvto, mvto*.

"Exploring the Depths of Creation and Meaning" originally appeared in *Terrain.org: A Journal of the Built & Natural Environments*, September 10, 2006. "You Might As Well Dance" was originally published in the winter 2008 issue of *Humanities INTERVIEW*; reprinted with permission of the Oklahoma Humanities Council. "The Craft of Soul Talk" is reprinted by permission of the Howard County Poetry and Literature Society, www.hocopolitso.org, and the *Little Patuxent Review*, www.littlepatuxentreview.org.

"Preface for *She Had Some Horses*" is used by permission of W. W. Norton & Company, Inc. "Afterword from *The Delicacy and Strength of Lace*" is reprinted with permission of Graywolf Press, Minneapolis, Minnesota, www.graywolfpress.org, from *The Delicacy and Strength of Lace: Letters Between Leslie Marmon Silko and James Wright*, edited by Anne Wright. "In Honor of Patricia Grace" was first published in *World Literature Today* 83.3 (May–June 2009): 34–36; reprinted by permission. "I Used to Think a Poem Could Become a Flower" originally appeared in *Ploughshares*, December 2004.

Grateful acknowledgment is also made to the following: *Triplopia, The Drunken Boat, Southern Scribe, El Molino Press, albuquerqueARTS, Multicultural Review*, and UCLA's *Indigenous People's Journal of Law, Culture and Resistance*.

"Breakthrough over Michigan Dunes." © Joy Harjo

Interviews

Becoming the Thing Itself

[Interview with *Triplopia*, 2005]

Joy Harjo knows noise.

Explore her writing and you'll soon find it rich in the auditory imagery of dogs barking, the ground speaking, and the moon playing the horn. And yet, sounds do much more than play to the senses in Harjo's poetry.

I was first introduced to Harjo's voice through her poem, "She Had Some Horses," in Lucille Clifton's poetry class. By a careful reading of the poem, Clifton managed to guide her undergraduates through the repetition of the poem, the horse-running composition found in the rhythms of the words, and the end line which reverberated within us.

"There is music here," Clifton suggested, and indeed there was.

Joy Harjo knows noise.

Harjo has won many accolades and awards for her writing, including the William Carlos Williams Award, the American Indian Distinguished Achievement in the Arts Award, the Josephine Miles Poetry Award, the Mountains and Plains Booksellers Award. She has won fellowships from the National Endowment for the Arts, the Arizona Commission on the Arts, and the Witter Bynner Foundation. She holds a B.A. from the University of New Mexico, an M.F.A. from the University of Iowa, and an honorary doctorate from Benedictine College. In 2003–2004, she won dual awards, Writer of the Year and Storyteller of the Year from Wordcraft Circle of Native Writers and Storytellers for her book, *How We Became Human: New and Selected Poems 1975–2001*, and her CD, *Native Joy for Real*. Most recently, Wordcraft Circle awarded her the title of 2005 Writer of the Year— Film Script, for *A Thousand Roads*, which she wrote for the National Museum of the Native American.

She is an artist in more ways than one, as she is poet, songwriter, screenwriter, children's writer, musician, and storyteller. And yet for all of her degrees, awards and accolades, she still runs across those who do not feel her writing is considered poetry.

Joy Harjo knows noise.

We recently had the privilege of catching up with Joy when we discussed the fusion of oral and written poetry, the responsibility of the poet, and the way music penetrates us all . . . .

You started out painting, yes?

Yes, I started out painting when I was young and often think about returning to it. I never quite developed it. I eventually leaped over to poetry.

And now you've been working with music for quite some time, as well as screenplays.

Music was probably my first love, but I didn't start working on it until the last fifteen years or so. I've written prose, and in fact, have a book way overdue at Norton. The contract is for a memoir, but memoir sounds so pretentious to me. It's actually a book of stories, some of it as memoir. At the moment I'm working on a show, something that will combine all of the above. And yes, screenplays, too. A screenplay I cowrote for the National Museum of the American Indian, *A Thousand Roads*, just premiered at Sundance.

There's a 1993 interview with Marilyn Kallet, in which Kallet asks if you regretted the decision to give up painting, and asked what poetry could do that painting couldn't, and you answered that it allows you to "Speak directly in a language that was meant to destroy us." Do you find yourself attracted to that particular challenge?

As an artist, I don't really think about all that—being interviewed also engages the creative. You know, you have to come up with answers for interviewers. [laugh] But yeah, you do it because it absolutely moves you. What attracted me to poetry was language, was basically sound. Poetry is a sound art. Oral poetry is experienced directly as sound art. Poetry in books is sound art but for the most part has lost the original link to performance. Now performance poetry has become a pejorative term. Poetry was here long before Mr. Gutenberg, scrolls, or any other book-like means of transporting the word. What enticed me about poetry was being able to hold in my hands and in my heart these small pieces of meticulous and beautiful meaning. It was like reclaiming the soul, or giving the soul a voice.

When you talk about your first encounter with music, you describe it as being drawn into the music on an almost physical level. There are a lot of other instances in which memory seems to be accompanied by the same mixing of senses. Is this part of the process for you?
I guess so. I don't like to think about it too much. You know? [laugh] Because when I start thinking too much, it gets in the way and some-times even just writing what I have to do is like going through a ritual to get rid of all the literal and linear and hierarchical stuff of the West-ern world, and I have to just let that go. My first experience of music in this world was through my mother's singing voice. I have a very, very faint memory of that experience while in the womb, and then it became the center of my world, especially in the formative years, when my mother was writing songs and singing for country swing bands, jukeboxes in truck stops where she worked, the radio, guitar players at the house. Music was and is my body. I don't think I ever felt a separation between music and my body. Words make bridges but music penetrates.

In reading your poetry, I find myself immediately thinking in terms of dynamicism.
Yes, that appears to be the consensus. I've collaborated with an as-tronomer, Stephen Strom: his photographs, my poetic prose pieces. His astronomical study is on the birth of stars. Poetry also concerns rigorous studies, of the human soul, which is directly connected to Strom's studies. We all appear to struggle in this universe. Poetry is basically another discipline and provides a structure for understand-ing the world. Science is a religion. Its world is mechanistic. Some philosophical strands of American and European poetry are similar, based on a mechanistic world, and more theoretical. To dip down into the soul is to get dirty. The more theoretical, the more removed it can become, and then you lose a relationship between the soul and the

world. You talk at it rather than move with it. I'll never forget my first day of teaching at the University of Colorado, Boulder. Reg Saner was a professor there. He introduced himself and came into my office. Said that he believed there were two kinds of poets; he called them Jacob and Esau poets, Jacob implying the refined and Esau the hairy wild man. He considered me of the second sort, primitive. Seems to me this becomes a pejorative kind of naming though he may not have meant it directly that way. The way I took it at that time was as a question: what is such a primitive poet doing in such a refined place?

And that connection between the soul and the world is important to you in your poetry?
To me, that's what poetry is. The communication with the soul is important to me, and maybe this, too, is considered primitive!

There's communication going on here.
Right.

In a couple of previous interviews, you've mentioned the idea of the fusion of oral and written as a new literature. How do you see this manifesting itself in your work?
Well, I think it is on *Native Joy for Real*. I consider singing, the saxophone, and poetry the blending of the oral and written. My early poems were short, lyrical statements usually fastened around one image. Then, they grew as my concept of poetry and vision grew. Being a mother of young children influenced the form. Then as the children grew, so did spaces of time in which to write. The lines grew longer, the vision deeper. The first experimentation I did with the interweaving of the oral with written was in *The Woman Who Fell From the Sky*. By the time I got those poems, I was trying to figure out how to make a book reflect an oral experience of poetry, in written form. Hence, the prose pieces in between the poems. They were another kind of experience that replicated, I felt, the experience of the performance of the poems. It's not the first time it was done. Evers' and Molina's *Yaqui Deer Songs* used this technique, and they referred to Leslie Silko's *Storyteller*. I wanted the experience of the book to mimic my oral presentations, which often have commentary preceding the

poems. *A Map to the Next World* expanded that concept. Maybe it doesn't work. Adding a saxophone takes you so far outside the written pages of a book, it's blasphemy!

How has a loss of credibility, for mixing genres, expressed itself, and how do you see such a reaction reflecting upon the world of poetry?
When you perform or sing or add a saxophone to your poetry, it's taken from the realm of literary art to performance art, and performance art is a pejorative term. Recently I came upon a blog written by someone who had come to a performance in Ojai that included Galway Kinnell, Suzanne Lummis, Lawrence Ferlinghetti, and me. She was a very good writer, kind of edgy, edgy academic. She trashed me and was very pleased with her erudite opinion. What I was doing wasn't real poetry. What did singing and saxophone have to do with it? She and others like her feel that the music is getting in the way of poetry. And if you read poetry a particular way, then I suppose it is. It's not supposed to be sung, and it's not supposed to have other kinds of accompaniment, or you're destroying the integrity of the written word. The words and text exist without you. That is one reality of poetry, a fixed, flat-planed reality.

In another interview, you mentioned that the division between music and poetry is not something that really has substance in some Native American traditions. In listening and reading your work, especially "Woman Hanging from the 13th Floor," and comparing them and seeing the revisions that had been done from one to the other, what was your process?
When I turned the poem into a song I trimmed about half of the poem, then added a hook line, chorus, and other musical kinds of elements.

What sort of things do you find demanding this sort of revision?
There's a difference between a spoken phrase and a sung phrase. And at the root is rhythm. It's been a primary creative spark for me, even before the music was added, or dropped in where it was always meant to be. Repeating elements are pleasing to the ear, or can be. In "Woman Hanging from the 13th Floor," "Set me free" in one verse is "Set us free," in the next, and in another "Set them free." It works, I

think. I didn't need these repeating elements in a poem, but the song needed them. The music fits right around other poems, as if I'd written them to include the music at some future point. This integration has been a long time coming. My first effort was *Furious Light*, a tape produced and distributed by a Washington, D.C., organization, Watershed Foundation. It's no longer available. I don't even have a copy anymore. Several prominent Denver jazz musicians performed on it, including Laura Newman and Eric Gunnison. The next was my formation of the band, Poetic Justice, which was first just Susan Williams and me, then her brother, John, then Will Johnson, and later Richard Carbajal. I spoke the poems on that project, which resulted in a CD of music, *Letter from the End of the Twentieth Century*. I learned to play saxophone on that album, played soprano and alto. My singing voice began to evolve and on the next project I learned to sing. The writing too has been affected. Three of the songs on *Native Joy for Real* are written as songs. The rest were poems first, and I suppose continue to be poems. It's a process and continues to be a process.

One of your most recent books, A Map to the Next World, *makes use of the same alternation between prose and poetry you mentioned in* The Woman Who Fell From the Sky.
Right. The book consciously leaps between the two. One is to be reminiscent of an oral act, the other more written.

And often the two inform each other. Some of the connections are more explicit, and some are less, but in one poem, "Returning from the Enemy," it seems to hit a real focus. The entire poem takes its form in exactly this way, and toward the end of the book, there's a final poem, "In the Beautiful Perfume and Stink of the World," in which you have two poems that are braided together.
That weaving informs the whole shape of the book and occurs at many levels, a kind of oral and written call-and-response, or the linear stacked next to the mythic. There's the overall book, then "Returning from the Enemy" mimics this shape within a longer poem, and then the shape occurs within the final poem, "In the Beautiful Perfume and Stink of the World." This was my original choice for the name of

the book, by the way, but my editor vetoed it—didn't like the word "stink" in the title. Found it repugnant. But to my thinking, it's part of this world, and now seems to be very much a part of this world. Anyway, within that poem, there is that back and forth, so that form is at work on three levels.

"Returning from the Enemy." That title is a reference to a Native American ceremony, is that correct?
Yes. A lot of native cultures have such ceremonies. The poem is intended to work as an actual ceremony for cleansing someone who has gone off to war—and certainly going out into the world can be going to war—and seen and participated in atrocities. Of course, seeing is a kind of participating. You are present at the moment. And what you've seen and taken in is dangerous—to the mind, body, soul, and spirit—and can infect everyone, not just in the present moment but through all time. Much of the monster we are witnessing now in America was given life with the first massacres. So basically the poem is a cleansing ceremony. And to be clean of something you have to go back to the root.

In this poem, this isn't a literal war, it's basically a war in terms of culture, correct?
Yes, it is a cultural war I'm addressing here. Violence informs all aspects of it. The source of much of this violence is a fundamentalist stance, a relentless stance in which one opinion or experience of religion, education, or culture is deemed the only one, and anything different is an enemy. Forcing language use is violent and disturbs the root of a people, both the afflicted and the perpetrator.

Your own poetry is often described as a 'poetry of witness,' thus suggesting that conceptions of history are quite central to your work. Do you see the primary aim of history, and by extension, a poetry of witness, to be similar to that of a cleansing ceremony?
I don't know about making a direct analogy between a cleansing ceremony and poetry of witness. Certainly poetry of witness can act as an element in a cleansing ceremony, or a series of poems could be ceremo-

nial in intent. I'm not sure what you're asking. Cleansing can be one part of a larger process of acknowledgment, preparation, recounting, and so on.

Well, for example, one of the threads of thought, in "Returning from the Enemy," is a comparison between the mythological and the everyday ways in which we see ourselves and others. For example, you write, "When my father remembered he was descended from leaders, he was ashamed he'd hit his wife, his baby. When I was the baby I did not know my father as a warrior, I knew him as an intimate in whose face I recognized myself." This comparison between mythological figures and real life, how do you think that informs the process you're describing in "Returning from the Enemy"?

I tenderly and reluctantly stepped into the place of that poem, didn't want to, but while in New Smyrna Beach could not deny what I was seeing forming directly in front of me, in a place known by my people before we were moved further and further west into what is now called Oklahoma. History became present and known. The micro and macro views are mirrors and they were fiercely reflecting there. I mean, we go out into the world and we encounter, but the world is also inside us. And we're inside the world, and within that configuration, all of this takes place in one space. There might be a distance, and there might be an intimate closeness, but it all takes place in the same space. Lately, I've been exploring how everything occurs within the same space at the same time, a thought akin to principles of quantum physics: each moment is layered and present. Being able to discern this is another matter. Poetry is a means.

You spoke, once, about your grandmother, I think it was, knowing the color of a general's dog, and how this informs your own sense of what is historical.

Yes, the dog belonged to my great-great-etc-great grandfather, Monah-wee, who was one of the major leaders of my tribe. He often turns up in the pages of history books, but these are the kind of details that are deleted—these heighten the meaning and lend context.

Memory, and the way it shapes our approach to history, is a very important concept for you, yes?

Right, because I think that memory is active. It's an active thing and it kind of twists through present, past, and future. I thought I knew what memory was/is, but I've been wrestling with that concept. Maybe there's human memory, which is flawed by emotional recall, point of view, etc, and then there's the memory of stones, which is closer to eternal but still flawed by lack of ability to move freely, and then over-memory, the ocean of all memories. For me, memory isn't situated in the past, but moves about freely. We can catch hold of it. And some of it is born within us, probably located somewhere in that DNA spiral. For instance, what if we take Monahwee and the example of the little black dog. We have the stories of him, or the memories of him, that are intimately connected because of family connections, and those family connections are kept solid because of the stories we continue to tell of him, and of that little black dog, and the stories of him basically able to bend time, when he traveled, and other stories. That's how we know him, through those intimate particulars. This memory was carried from Monahwee to his son, then daughter, then daughter, then my great-aunt Lois Harjo, who told me, and I wonder how it's changed through this chain of human rememberers. Most of us are pretty eccentric in our remembering. But, the image is there, nonetheless, and links to other stories about his ability to communicate with animals, including his horses. And because we speak them—and because there's power in speaking, there's power in thinking, and in dreaming and re-membering, because it makes energy—it makes real energy. And every time you think, dream, speak, or write of someone or something, it gives power and makes connections. And even when you think about your enemies, same thing. This is about a process of linking. The connection is dynamic. Our family has the memory of Monahwee, as does the tribe. And then there's the memory of Menawa (pronounced differently in Alabama) whose McKenney-Hall image is presented next to Andrew Jackson at the Battle of Horseshoe Bend Monument in Alabama. There, he's an image of defeat, of takeover, and he represents the end of Native presence in the area. I'll never forget performing at Auburn University. When I announced that I was the granddaughter of Monahwee, they gasped. It was an immense gasp. I was suddenly a ghost appearing in front of them. All these years my relatives and I had been presumed dead. So that Monahwee, or Menawa, as they called him there, was a flat figure in history. He was a part of a process of colonization. He wasn't real. And that's the difference, because where I come from, that particular spirit lives. Your spirit can travel back— or forwards, depending—and connect, because it's there and part of you. I believe that history contracts and expands, depending. I can see Monahwee's spirit evident in the children, grandchildren—it grows itself. Frightening to think about what is growing, what we are given birth to as our actions and thoughts leap from us. [laugh] You know? [laugh] We're all grown from each other. We're part of a process, of a root system. I think ideas are given form in that same manner. Even theories are a creative act.

You almost get the sense, in this conception of it, that memory is a sentient being, and that the division between past, present, and future is useful, in a practical sense, but not essentially real. You've mentioned, a number of times, that when we speak, when we dream and think, this has power, it puts energy out there and changes the world. This poem, "Returning from the Enemy," ends with somebody who is being severely tortured, and who continues to sing throughout it. How does that fit in for you, do you think?
This image, this story was taken from a story that appeared in the *New Yorker* on a massacre in El Salvador. Men were taken out and shot and women and children herded into a church and burned. Other women and girls were hunted down in the fields, then raped and killed. The one survivor told the story of how she watched all of this, hidden in the field. The most beautiful girl of all of them was singled out for heavy and violent rape. In the middle of her degradation she sang. She went down singing. To take what was meant to destroy her and turn it into a song is one of the most powerful acts I have been witness to, and I was witness to it in a story that was printed in the *New Yorker*. Funny to think of the *New Yorker* magazine as being a carrier of memory. But it is. And it was, for me. And in the context of my poem/story sequence, which references a historical span of much degradation, killing, and theft, it made sense. It does make quite a leap, in the context, and that could, in the end, be an inherent weakness in the sequence.

Maybe the singing will help shift the pattern, the reaction to the pattern, and maybe that's behind my singing of the poems. The poem/story sequence is really about facing the ruins of colonization in my family, myself. The overriding voice is female, includes many different ages of female. Historically, there are no female voices, and especially no female Native voices. The only two who appear are Pocahontas, and she has no direct voice but remains as an image, as a colonized figure in her English clothes. And there's Sacajawea, who has a voice because of her link to two white explorers, Lewis and Clark. We don't hear her voice. Most Native stories weren't and aren't recorded on paper. There are many reasons for that, but overall there's a basic mistrust of the written word, as our experience with it has been writing as a colonizing tool. And women weren't respected by the colonizers. Males wrote and made history and still do. Stories, songs, and poems exist more so in the space of memory. And to know them you have to have an intimate relationship with the tribe and be literally part of the context of the tribe. The power of the written word is access, and a different kind of movement, which also promotes a different kind of remembering. So, in "Returning from the Enemy," the speaker is female. She holds the father in that voice, carries memory.

To find memory, or desire, or some other emotional force, coming across in your poems as living creatures seems so important to what is being said. Do you think the process, in more mechanistic approaches, of trying to make things still, and believing that in doing that that you will gain more knowledge about it, is part of the problem?
Well, it's always been strange to me that in order to understand something you dissect it and you take the pieces apart. And certainly that can be a useful process, I suppose, but then you study the pieces, but you don't look at the force that's animating the whole being, and you don't see how the pieces are connected first, though the logic of how everything hangs together is telling of the immensity of the creative, dynamic source. Science to me is really about studying the pieces but disregarding the life force itself.

There's a deep connection, in your poetry, between memory and responsibility. Could you tell me a little more about that?

The word "responsibility" in terms of poetry tends to freak out the American poet. The idea that we have a responsibility for what we say often feels like a steel jacket to the American Dream poet, where everything is available to you, and the land is yours for the taking. There's still sort of that attitude, I think, with poetry, or even with anything Indian, where it's there for the taking, and it just doesn't really work that way. I keep remembering a quote from Luci Tapahonso, and she said it in Navajo, but I can't remember the Navajo: "The sacred is on the tip of the tongue." The Disney American mind believes it can get something for nothing, that riches and fame are the end goal and describe success. But things don't come free. There's a payment for everything that you do. If you write something, something has to be offered in return. And that's part of the dynamic process. You can't just take. But there's a whole process to that, there's also giving back, and I think that's part of the responsibility, too. Ideas and images, in the way they come through, they're given to you, you're part of the process. Certainly writing is a way of giving it back. But there is a larger responsibility. Certainly I write because it delights me, and that's at the root of any artist, that the form, and moving within that form, delights you. But I'm also aware that there are certain things I can't write about, mostly ceremonial. But not to have permission to write about them doesn't make me feel stymied or censored. It's just that there are some things that are sacred, and beyond writing.

And that just don't go into words.
And some places are sacred, not meant for non-ceremonial or non-tribal members. Many Americans just don't accept this, though they certainly wouldn't want us putting highways across their altars and pulpits. "I'm an American, I can do anything I want. I can write about anything I want. I can give myself an Indian name if I want." And so on.

Acknowledging that there's a responsibility to be silent, in some spaces, would you also say there is a time when a poet is charged with a responsibility to speak?
There's that great poem from the bible in Ecclesiastes that encapsulates this: "A time to be born, a time to die, a time for everything under

the seasons," that the Byrds made into a song so long ago. For poetry, silence is a tool that is just as important as words. I believe the role of the poet is truthteller. And you follow the poem to the truth. You cannot commandeer the poem. It doesn't work that way. Writing is about a tenth of what poetry is—maybe another part of this question is censorship, that is, most Americans believe that they should have access to anything in the world they want; it's their birthright as Americans, and they are insulted when they are turned away from a ceremony, or told that certain texts or songs are dangerous and belong to certain families or people. They can write about anything they want and it has nothing to do with integrity. Sometimes integrity means being silent, about particular songs or texts because they are to be opened only in certain places or under certain conditions because otherwise they won't have life, or might diminish or endanger life.

I'm interested in how dynamicism affects your approach to poetry, because there are people out there for whom dynamicism, in poetry, means never revising, and that's clearly not the case with your work.
No, I think you have a responsibility to craft to the best of your ability. I think you have a responsibility to build something that's well-crafted. Something that will stand the test of time or the test of weather, doubt [laugh]—all of that. Many of my younger students or less experienced students still have a resistance to craft. They hang on to the first draft as their only draft because they are still amazed that they gave birth to anything. And what they've given birth to isn't always poetry. We all have a responsibility to craft. Allen Ginsberg had this famous quote, "First thought, best thought." The first thought might carry the seed of the thing, but the first swipe of sandpaper doesn't necessarily make the most elegant sculpture, and maybe I'm after a certain kind of elegance in the middle of the wreck. And then I complicate the wreck with a saxophone and singing. Maybe some people just have a different approach, and sometimes it works for them. I don't go to contests or anything, though I have been invited to perform at some performance slam poetry events, and there I am at the *HBO Def Poetry Jam*, and it's like I've stepped out of another time and place. When I'm in those spaces I know I'm not a performance poet. My stuff is resonating at another level. It's not hard, fast, or punchy and showy. I'm not going

a hundred and fifty miles into a wall of excitement. I'm not riding the ride for sheer entertainment.

So in terms of crafting, I'm wondering how this dynamicism informs the revision process.
I'm still not sure how to answer this. I can scramble around and pull up "Fear Song," or "I Give You Back," as it was first called—the poem was larger than me when I wrote it in my mid- to late twenties. The poem has its own life. Even though you're bringing in the thinking part of the mind, to help craft, you still have the other part involved. It's almost like the poem is there and you kind of scrape away the things that don't work to unearth it.

Do you see the process of revision taking the poet further away from the truth, or bringing them closer?
I see revision as the road to the deepest heart of the poem. It's what writing poetry is about. I chip away and don't always know what I'm going to find. I've had some poems appear almost, but not quite, done, and others I wrangle with for years. But I've never had a poem just stand up in one draft and say "Here I am."

Well, revision isn't necessarily a written process, either.
No, it's not always written, and sometimes the revision goes on before the pen hits the paper or we tap it out on the screen. Li Young Lee once said that he revises long before the pen hits the paper . . . he works on it before it becomes physical.

I wanted to ask a couple of questions about "the crow and the snake."
I very much enjoyed this piece. I felt it, on one level, as a political alle-gory, but by using the snake in the way you do, are you playing with the Judeo-Christian creation myth?
I hadn't really considered the Christian creation story analogy, but it works. There are levels to the piece, and then the impetus. I wanted to see what would happen to the overrun of birds who had designated the backyard as their gathering place. There were often literally hundreds who appeared there. So it started with a big old rubber snake. But of course, that's the literal. Christianity, of the sort practiced in the

United States, ascribes the fall of humans to a snake, and a woman! In a Mvskoke reading, a snake in a tree would immediately tell you something powerful and strange was afoot, so to speak, and you would get away. Eating of the tree of knowledge could give you power but it would require tests and fasting. Adding an underworld animal to a middle world being, a tree complicates it. The myth doesn't embrace, however. It excludes the power of the snake, the power of women, and the power of the earth mother. And it's a crow who comes back and puzzles over the story and finds a different conclusion. And notice I link "who" with crow, not "that" or "it." A relationship is made here, not the one of Adam dominating the world and having the power to dominate. That crow had such depth—could have been a poet crow!

That question of domination, as opposed to engagement, is something that shows up in a lot of your work, and it seems to be at the root of poetry, for you. What practical steps do you take to engage the world? Or are those steps practical?
I think that a lot of it is very, very basic. I suppose it's—if you were to have a Mvskoke Creek University, you know, that's 101. I noticed a shift in my practice of being a human when I was seven years old and went to public school. Actually, this is when I started going to church, too, lured by cookies and Kool-Aid. There was no place for who I had been, or who I was, except the artist or the singer in art or music classes. I went from a world of music, a world in which I could see things, in which I could see the movements of energy between people and plants, or animals. A very engaged and alive relationship with this world we're in. In school the world I was taught was relatively flat, but brilliant in conception and variety. And in that world there were no females, there were no Indians, and even though half the class was Indian we read that there were no more Indians. In this world only the mental and rote learning had a place. Except in art and music classes, which I loved.

In the first poem of A Map to the Next World, *"Songline of Dawn," you seem to be exploring a particular take on our relationship with the gods. There was one line that struck me in particular, "Protect them, oh gods of the scarlet light / who love us fiercely despite our acts of stupidity / our utter failings.* " *My first reaction to this line was to ask myself how the Judeo-Christian tradition might shift if one were to reconceive of its god as being fallible. In the spiritual world you're describing in your work, how do you think the gods might be seen regarding their own fallibility? Are they less than perfect?*

I think so. In the poem "A Map to the Next World," a star was once a human, or had a very human experience, and possibly failed. If the Sun was perfect it wouldn't be here either. [laugh] I've been called a Buddha-ist, but it's very Mvskoke, or Creek. And then I have my own track—we all do in our approach. Traditional people in my tribe have always allowed for that—it defines us as humans. I guess I do have a little bit of a problem with organized religions, generally, but everything has its place. It's not just the commercial aspects, but the forced-enrollment-or-you-go-to-hell aspects. Doesn't make common sense, or even uncommon beautiful sense.

How do you understand the relationship to god changing, if that god is conceived of as being fallible?

I think we can only experience god, for the most part, by the size of our minds or by the size of our hearts. Every once in a while there can be a point or moment of grace. Like an incredible poem you read or hear [laugh], you know? That suddenly opens everything up. Or a piece of art, or a small but incredible act of kindness in somebody that opens everything up. Or experiencing someone's death with them, or experiencing somebody's birth with them. We are then opened to our utter humanness, which paradoxically links us to our experience of god. But then god is certainly that, is through everything, I mean, it's the life force. It's that life force that animates absolutely everything.

What creation myth did you grow up with, as a member of the Mvskoke tribe?

The most predominant creation story is Christian. Probably more than half the tribe is Christian, so the major story involves Adam and Eve and the Garden of Eden. We have more than one version of a Mvskoke creation story because the tribe is made up of several smaller groups. I've heard several versions, from several different entities within the tribe. I've been pulling everything together, trying to make sense of it all, and in my family it appears that our tribal creation story might have us coming thousands of years ago from Polynesia, up from South America into Mexico, and then over. I believe current anthropology might even back this up. Volcanoes figure into the story, as does the Pacific Ocean.

In the Mvskoke tradition, Rabbit is the trickster, is that right?
Yes, and Rabbit, the trickster, was there at the beginning of creation. And Rabbit is neither male nor female. Neither is the overall deity or overseer of all creation. Christianity invests heavily in making all the rulers male. One of the first things the churches did was to change or destroy our narratives. Female deities were turned into male, if they survived the destruction. A trinity of a father, son, and holy ghost leaves out any female presence or power at the beginning of creation. Strange. In this world there can be no creative power without the female force. Mary was always there as an afterthought, and was only there as a virgin, not as a fully grown woman [laugh], so to speak, and not as a female deity or power. So that premise, for me, is quite faulty. And it doesn't work for me that, again, a male was given dominion over the land. Everything comes down to common sense. It doesn't make sense. Earth is larger than humans in size and consciousness. We're guests on this earth. Humans are just part of a larger creation. If it so happens we were given dominion, or males were—and I don't believe this at all and it's one reason I walked away from the church at thirteen—then we certainly won't have it next time around. We've done nothing but rape the earth of its resources and don't even turn around. We forget to say thank you.

On that same line, to go back to the poetry here, the process of creation suggests for some, a creator/creation relationship similar to that relationship conceived of between god and universe. Do you see these two relationships as being similar?
Yes, I do. I believe that we are creators in every moment, with every thought, word and deed. I don't imagine myself as god creating a universe. [laugh] I guess I should say that. I don't think of that literally. There's a certain immensity, or eternalness about god and creation, and then here's the little human poet creating the human poem. So

there's another step, or a few steps, left out. But the impulse is very similar.

In light of the similarities between these relationships, what are your views regarding the possibility of perfection within the discipline of poetry?
Well, I don't know that perfection follows humans around. This isn't the perfect world, though some moments are near perfect, and I've read some near-perfect poems. They haven't been mine. There are moments, but I don't know that humans are capable of perfection.

In previous interviews, you've made note of what appears to be a key difference between classical European conceptions of art and Native American conceptions of same, characterizing it as follows: "In a Native context art was not just something beautiful to put up on the wall and look at; it was created in the context of its usefulness for people." How do you see poetry being useful in the context of present day America?
Poetry doesn't appear to be useful or in use to mainstream America. It is the least-read genre, along with plays. And fewer and fewer people are buying books or going to the library. Yet, some people do read, continue to read, to take time to delve into questions of the soul, and how those questions are constructed. Poetry is very alive in oral venues: slam poetry, ceremonial poetry, song poetry. Performance poetry is usually wrapped around narrative, word play with a big hit of sensationalistic techniques. Some of it can be quite stunning and amazing. Patricia Smith is someone who straddles written and oral. Often it's poetry as testimony of the soul of these times. Much of it isn't pretty or rarified, but most life here isn't—I guess what I'm trying to say is that much of it appears to be urban, though the slam movement has made its way to the reservations, to Hopiland and Navajoland. Especially rap. As far as usefulness literally, I've written poems whose purpose is to move into the world and effect change. I've written a poem to get rid of fear. Another, "Rainy Dawn," becomes a poem to usher girlhood to womanhood transformation and to bring rain. I have a difficult time assembling some larger statement on the state of American

poetry. It's alive. We're alive and we're singing. The standards appear to be slipping, however—but, overall, written or oral, poetry describes the shape and size of the soul in America in these times.

On the question of written and oral forms of poetry, you've said, in the past, "I believe that written language was, in many ways, a devolution of the communication process. You lose human contact. With written communication, you gain the ability to lie more easily." Do you see the written word as a method of controlling others?

I think words, yes, have the ability to control. It depends on who's speaking them, it depends on the intent. I think of pure communication as communication beyond words. When there is nothing between speaker and audience, no misunderstandings, no lies, no hidden agendas—there's no need for translation. When we speak and are in the presence of each other, that is, poet and audience, for instance, there's also communication that happens beyond words—the speaker and audience both are part of the poem, energetically, literally. Books are wonderful inventions, as is the ability to translate poems to the page, and read them later . . . as if they were freeze-dried. I love being able to carry books around and have them available for reading whenever I want—but something is lost here, the context, the voice, the performance. We get farther and farther away from each other with each step of so-called progress, yet, paradoxically we are brought together from far distances. But of course, the intent can get lost in context. Words are an expression of spirit—and poetry is written/spoken expression at its most distilled. Maybe in this country for most people the link has been broken between poetry and an individual's intimate experience of poetry. And in my tribe and with many indigenous people, words on paper are suspect because they've been used to sign away land and take away children. They're still being used in courts of law to steal. And people who write are usually seen as making money off their writing or off the tribe by their writing, so they're suspect, their motives are suspect.

There's an early Noni Daylight poem, "Someone Talking," in which Noni is describing a feeling and she can't think of the word, and then she thinks of the word and it's "Milky Way." And that's the word for what she's feeling. This particular theme comes through a number of times, where you seem to be comparing experience with words. It seems that you're saying that your idea of poetry is much broader than what many people would allow it to be.

Oh, I think so. I'm grappling to express what might be a different experience of poetry, or maybe it's the same, but different words, a slightly different context.

To the point that it seems like the stars themselves could be described as a poem.

Yes, at some point, and maybe the ultimate purpose of the poem, is to become the thing itself, rather than naming it.

Do you think they're a better poem?

Sometimes, yes. [laugh]

There's one image—the Sandia Mountains, as seen from the Albuquer-que airport—that shows up in your poetry over and over again.

The Sandia Mountains for years were my guardians. They were the magnetic center as I lived in New Mexico, mostly Albuquerque, for most of my life. I'm excited that I will return there this fall and every fall to teach a semester at the University of New Mexico.

These show up way back in What Moon Drove Me to This, *in the poem "I am a Dangerous Woman," which describes going into an airport security check.*

And that was way back when those checkpoints were really benign. But I didn't consider them benign then. They were obstructions to free movement, and again, it made no sense as 99.99 percent of us aren't terrorists. If I had to write that poem now it would be twice as long and very angry.

In one of the prose pieces in A Map to the Next World, *"sudden aware-ness," the same place shows up. You're talking about what might be going on in your mind while dying, and how some of the thoughts coming to you, stupid things like the Pepsodent jingle.*

[laugh] I know all of those, that's horrifying to me. You know how you can get stuck on a jingle, or some kind of meaningless repetition.

And it just carries you on out. [laugh] But in this piece, you have the place between the security checkpoint and the plane as the last image. I've always had a problem with transition points, for example, before the checkpoint and after, borders of countries, the place between waking and sleeping, dreaming and waking, starting to write and writing, and so on. I have a relatively new poem, now a song, inspired by watching the sun rise in the Albuquerque airport. It's a poem, "Morning Song," on *Native Joy for Real*: "The red dawn is rearranging the earth, thought by thought, beauty by beauty." It's a song now.

Does that mention the Albuquerque airport?
No it doesn't, though that's where it started. This is an example of where the personal story doesn't really matter: the poem, or song, is as it is at that moment, but it wouldn't have happened without Albuquerque, the airport, the impending birth of a granddaughter, the impending death of a beloved Sioux man.

The things that have happened in America to change those security checks, how have they affected your writing?
Maybe what I've seen is what's been underground, what's been bubbling beneath the surface, or boiling beneath the surface of American consciousness all along, it's just been opened. You think about what this society is coming to when the children kill each other. These killings are a terrible poem, a comment on the state of the American soul. This is capped off by the very raw and recent Red Lake killings by a child. What have we come to when children are killing each other? The killings are a cry of desperation on behalf of the family, the nation, the child. They are cries of defeat. This is connected to the ability to understand and create metaphor really being lost. Most language use is for buying or selling, or for commenting on manufactured stories, stories that don't make connections between the children and their families, their families and communities, between smaller and larger communities of all life forms.

Do you see these "cries of defeat" as being individual, or do you think it's wider than that?

The individual is linked to family, is linked to clan (which in my tribe makes certain relationships with plants, animals, people), and is linked to larger groups like town, city, state, country, then earth, then planetary system. All are occurring at the same time and are part of the intimate structure of a human being. Last night I was speaking with a Pueblo healer friend of mine about the earth medicines. The trees want to share as do the plants. And when we share with anyone, whether they are plant, animal, mineral, we make a familial relationship, or maybe the word is we acknowledge it, because it's innately there. There are connections every which way, but it does distill itself in the intimate human experience.

You linked violence between children with the loss of the ability to understand and create metaphor. Do you see our ability to engage metaphor as being an antidote for violence?

To engage metaphor is to be inside these innate connections between human, sky, earth. Then, we *are* earth or *as* earth. We are not standing at a distance looking at earth and then selling earth. Violence occurs with distancing. Many of those coming up in the age of television and movies as the prime storytellers feel no connection between themselves and the ability to make stories. Violence isn't real. But it's ever present. I was recently talked into going to the American Hollywood movie *Mr. and Mrs. Smith*. I knew better. It was a vehicle to show off two American movie stars, to make money. There was no story to speak of—the movie consisted of many head and body shots and a barrage of special effects: violence. The stars come out of tremendous violence untouched, or rather, retouched makeup, clothes. They win in the end, they always do. There's no connection between this and their lives in these times. And no one can ever live up to the beauty of these humans whose images have been manipulated by light and makeup. Violence is part of the human landscape. The old stories, fairy tales, animal tales and such all include violence—but there are intimate connections between what occurs and meaning in our lives. Then you add being an Indian teenager to the equation and most likely you don't look like these people, you don't belong to the overriding story except as an

Indian. And every day you're reminded of this. The suicide rate is outrageous in Indian country. Many deaths that aren't counted as suicide are probably covert suicide, like car wrecks.

Do you think there's been a real change in atmosphere, or would you argue that it's just a more vocal expression of what was already there? Recently a friend who's been doing everything in her life she can think of to escape the truth of her history, her family, to duck under the pain, with smoke, drink, lovers, the usual—made a small movement to get up from a sitting position, from a slope near a river about two in the morning, and her knee literally exploded. Suddenly. She didn't fall, there was no apparent impact, just the usual movement associated with standing up. I told her, it didn't just happen. This has been in the works for the last few years as she's carried immense grief, from the death of an important relative-ally, the death of her childhood, the pressures she's carried from her family's expectations and guilting. It's like termites eating out a piece of wood, then the house falls; 9/11 is like that. The United States has been involved for years, since the takeover of this country, in imperialistic forays into the world for territory, for resources, goods, workers. The bruise grows, then suddenly there's an attack. It appears to have "just happened." It didn't. That's not to say that I agree with it. Many, many innocent lives were destroyed. We were all changed. It was the built-up charge of suppression, and maybe deals gone bad between U.S. leadership and particular families in the Middle East. And so it appeared to happen suddenly, but there's a trail that goes way back, like roots. They lead directly from the event to the White House, to Saudi Arabia, the heads of multinational corporations. I feel like I'm in a dysfunctional family in this country. We all see what's happening, but many are pretending to not see, because the truth appears so devastating. So they pretend nothing happened, or no, not our country, our daddy. We've found ourselves as participants in the children's story, *The Emperor's New Clothes*.

At the heart of the myth of the American Dream story is cowboys-and-Indians. It's dark against light, good against evil with the white guys or European/Christian ideas being the good and evil being the so-called primitive or earth ways and those who practice those ways, or have darker skin. And anyone who isn't Euro-Christian is an Indian.

The military not-so-code word for the battlefield in Iraq or during the Gulf War is/was Indian Country. The Iraqis are the Indians, the U.S. military the cowboys. This is the root assumption that underlies American education, most religious organizations. It shapes the process of thinking and being in this time and place. Classical traditions imply European, yet we have many classical traditions in this country: Navajo, Mvskoke, for instance. Cotton Mather called the Indians "devils." We're still being treated as devils. I never heard or saw the devil until I went to church. We are in the middle of religious wars, and the U.S. religious right is one of the main instigators. I grew up in Oklahoma. I know the story intimately! And because of the regime that's in place, those people have power. It's a false power, but a very earthly power. But power is a tricky thing. Try picking up a live wire. If you can handle it and plug it in you can light a city.

"There is music here," Clifton suggested. Indeed, there is. And within that music sings many messages. Be still for a moment. Listen.

Music, Poetry, and Stories

Returning to the Root Source

[Interview with Rebecca Seiferle, 2008]

There are, as it were, two different landscapes present in these poems you've given us: the landscape of Hawai'i, which seems a landscape of healing and blessing, and the landscape of the American West, which is preoccupied with the historical wounding of the Native American peoples and also has aspects of a more difficult healing through the blessing of song. Would you like to talk about the importance that place, those particular intersections of human reality with the earth, has in your work?

Lately I've been immersed in a revisioning, rethinking of my relationship to landscape. This is most definitely related to the dramatic shift in landscape and place that occurred when I left New Mexico, Oklahoma, (and even Los Angeles) for Hawai'i six years ago. I crossed the Pacific to an island nation. The shift was abrupt. Though I was familiar with the people and place of Hawai'i, to move there was another thing. I moved to be with someone with whom I have a close kinship and with whom I enjoy a sense of peacefulness. I also moved to the water, and took up outrigger canoe paddling. And since I was a child I have always wanted to be in the Pacific. I didn't really know too much about it but would always dream about Tahiti, Hawai'i, even New Guinea. What can happen, though, with such shifts, you come to know what you've left behind even more intimately because you have to imagine and remember intensely to bring it close. Sometimes you do that by writing, as Leslie Silko did when she wrote *Ceremony* while living in Ketchikan, Alaska, far from Laguna Pueblo. Ketchikan has one of the highest rainfall averages in the country. While it rained and rained, she wrote her desert home back around her. Hawai'i is a great refuge for my spirit. I paddle. I help out with horses. Practice singing and horn. And write music, poetry, and stories that always return me to the root source from those birthing places. I continue to feel that pull and connection to those lands which have nourished and challenged me on this journey. As I grow older those places grow larger and larger.

It seems to me that there is an opening in your Hawai'i poems to a greater sense of peacefulness and a feeling blessed by what is. Not that it wasn't present in your earlier work, but it seems to flower forth here in these poems. How has living in Hawai'i affected you?
Probably the largest shift in landscape is water. The island of O'ahu is relatively small. The Pacific is immense. I am learning water. And the water might be beautiful but it is also powerful and dangerous. When you go out in the water, you have to be aware and know that anything can happen. There are shifts in currents and weather. You might start out your paddle in flat water, then struggle on the way back with wind and breaking waves. The most peaceful moments have been out on the water just after dawn, with sea turtles alongside, and once in a while pods of dolphins. The most frightening was having a sudden rogue wave break over, a wave that could have broken the small canoe. It didn't, but threw me out of the boat. I made it back on and we got out of there. It's about learning to flow and not fight. I also like having my favorite fruits and flowers in the yard: mangos, papayas, bananas, hibiscus, coconut, and frangipani. I have a great love and respect for Hawaiian poetry, which isn't separated from dance and music. It's all together. Poetry, music and dance came into the world together. Will go out that way, together, too.

The Southwest is, of course, the most arid of environments, the depths of a long-ago vanished ocean. Do you feel moving to a world of water has allowed you more fluidity and fluency of poetic being?
I've always noted waterlines of the old oceans on the mesas and mountains in the Southwest. Often they are very visible. Too, I've often

imagined the skies there as oceans. But yes, when water is the prevailing influence everything in the atmosphere carries its essence of being.

There is an ease with the mythologies, the stories, of the Hawaiian people in these poems. Do you feel a natural affinity for these myths?
Despite the military takeover (the military controls and "owns" over 25 percent of the lands of Hawai'i) and the population growth of outsider groups, the overall cultural sense in Hawai'i is clearly Hawaiian. The myths, stories are still fluid and are present in the mountains, fields, rivers and oceans. They are in the names, the dances, in everything. They remind me of my own tribal stories.

I am particularly struck by the speaker's honest confrontation with her own anger, and turning away from it. Given the state of the world today, would you like to talk about how poetry has been a part of your turning away from "the war club" into song, which while it does not disavow the justified anger or deny the ways in which people have been afflicted, is another way of being?
Without poetry, without song, without dance I would not be alive. Nor would any of us. We come from root cultures in which song, poetry, stories, art was something that belonged to all of us. They were not "spectator sports," as they are mostly in this over-culture. Everyone sang, everyone, danced, made art. It was/is integral to being human. Now it seems reserved for the elite, for those who can afford the time. We need expression to feel connected, not just to our communities but to who we are down deep, past the eyes and the gullet, to the heart and the incredible depth past it.

You play the saxophone and perform your works with a band. How has performing music altered your sense of writing poetry? Do you feel there's a natural affinity between these arts, a complementary quality?
I've been working hard in the studio on my next CD, *Native Joy for Real*. I am singing on this album, playing horn, and doing some speaking of poetry. After this album I believe most of my energy will be more in the direction of music. Poetry has always felt a little lonely, needed some kind of accompaniment. And I've gone back, in a way, to

my roots, to the singing. That was the original impetus of the poetry, and of the sax, to find a way to sing. I still want my poems to stand up on their own.

Rebecca Seiferle was awarded a Lannan Literary Fellowship in 2004. Her fourth poetry collection, *Wild Tongue* (Copper Canyon, 2007) won the 2008 Grub Street National Book Prize in Poetry. Her previous poetry collections have won the Western States Book Award, a Pushcart prize, the Hemley and Bogin awards, the Writer's Exchange Award, and the National Writers' Union Prize. Seiferle is the founding editor and publisher of the online international poetry journal, *The Drunken Boat*, www.thedrunkenboat.com.

Exploring the Depths of Creation and Meaning

[Interview with Simmons Buntin, September 2006]

Barry Lopez recently said that critics, academics, and the media ask "questions about what I intended to do, to say, to achieve in my writing, as though the writing is intentional or purposive. They think that you sit down to write down what it is that you think about something. Writing does not work like this at all. I sit and write, and in the writing I am simply present—with the thought, the place, the idea. It arrives." Does your writing work in the same way, or do you approach writing as a particular project, with something particularly to say? As an American Indian, a woman, a global citizen, is there a continuous message you must relay?

I am in agreement with Barry. I am part of a larger process. I don't have control over it. I do have control (mostly) about being prepared, ready, and am willing to put in the time and commitment to crafting what is given. If I am going to give a message then I don't do it as a writer, poet, or songwriter. Doesn't mean that some message or sense isn't made of it all. I am driven to explore the depths of creation and the depths of meaning. Being Native, female, a global citizen in these times is the root, even the palette. I mean, look at the context: human spirit versus the spirits of the earth, sky, and universe. We are part of a much larger force of sense and knowledge. Western society is human-centric. We're paying the price of foolish arrogance, of forgetfulness.

While acknowledging that you have learned to respect various artistic genres and "those who have mastered them and brought them to another level of accomplishment," you have also said that "the creative stream isn't strictly bound by genres or expression." Books like A Map to the Next World: Poems and Tales, *provide an excellent example—alternating poems and tales to create a four-part story. When you were writing the poems and tales of this book, were they created in largely the same order as they appear in the book, or were the poems written separately—grouped—from the tales? Or perhaps differently altogether? Is there a difference in the construction of a mixed-genre collection versus a single genre? Should writing programs encourage more mixed or cross-genre writing, promoting or at least accounting for the ebb and flow of the creative stream?*

The poems were created separately and not in the order as they appear. The tales—some were created separately and most after I pulled together the shape of the book. What moved me to venture in that direction was to try for some kind of sense of orality in a written text. Written text is, to me, fixed orality. I tried this first in *The Woman Who Fell from the Sky*. Of course the poems can exist by themselves. They do not need explanations. The prose accompaniments are part of the overall performance. I expanded it in *Map*. . . . I am always aware of several voices and each has its own root of impulse and quality. The poetry voice exists in timelessness. When I try to force it to a contemporary arch tone—it fails me, though I did recently write a hip-hop type poem. Still, the voice had the same overarching tone and voice, a voice that is wiser than me. Then there's the more narrative voice—and it's more contemporary. Often my poetry voice is like a voice coming from stones . . . and so on. Each book is a different experiment or expression. *Secrets from the Center of the World* was my first mixed-genre book. Photographs by Stephen Strom and my poetic prose pieces were together in response to the landscape near the Four Corners area.

As far as writing programs teaching cross-genre—some encourage experimentation and some discourage any leaning past the middle line of form. It's up to each writer to find and follow his or her own direction. You will either have support, or you won't have support. And your vision might coincide with taste and it might not. Taste and movements come and go.

In the "classics" of modern American poetry, and often in the teach-
ing of poetry, poetry as literature is separate from music, both lyrics
and composition. While there is a certain music to poetry, and poetry
derives from the spoken word, the general conclusion has been: poetry
is not music and music is not poetry. Your work with your band Poetic
Justice, where you bring your poetry to music or alternatively music to
your poetry, suggests otherwise (for example, "She Had Some Horses"
in the book of the same name is also a song on the album Letter from
the End of the Twentieth Century*). What is the relationship between*
music and poetry, generally and in your work? Does the heritage of
music in American Indian culture provide for a bridge between the
two genres in your work, as opposed to the historical separation of
music and poetry in modern Western verse?

The roots of poetry lead to music. Music will often be found yearn-
ing for singers. Poetry is a sound art. I happened on the direct rela-
tionship between poetry and music when I realized that most of the
poetry in my tribe, and with most peoples of the world, isn't found in
books, it's oral. Then I began to consider how to make that bridge—I
didn't do so with a direct plan—it was a natural outgrowth of being a
contemporary Mvskoke poet who had picked up a saxophone. Poetic
Justice was just a start. I collaborated first with Susan M. Williams on
the music for "For Anna Mae Pictou Aquash." Then we added her
brother John to the band, a bass player, to round it out. Then it devel-
oped from there. For that configuration I read my poems, performed
sax, and helped create the songs. We had to find a crossing between
song structures and my poems. My poems don't usually behave and
conform to known structures—many are conscious hybrids. The same
goes with music.

Then after Poetic Justice (I disbanded Poetic Justice to go out on
my own with a band), I began singing and this demanded a different
shape to the poem. Some of my poems lend themselves to singing, like
"Grace" (featured on my last music album, *Native Joy for Real*), and
others to a mix of singing, speaking, and even a form of chant-singing.
I have written some songs as lyrics. There is a difference. I've trans-
formed some poems to lyrics. The singing voice demands a difference
in rhythm, pacing, beginning and end sounds. Right now I am work-

ing on translating some of my poems into the Mvskoke language, then into songs for singing. This is an ongoing process of discovery.

You have said, and many artists have echoed, that we are "within a dominant culture that doesn't value the artist." Indeed, public funding for art of all types continues to come under fire on a regular basis. Is it the artist's responsibility to work to change our culture so it does value the artist? Is the artist responsible for more even than that: for bearing witness, making public, and demanding action to resolve the inequalities of our world: social, economic, environmental, and otherwise? How do artists engender compassion, or even overarching compassion, as in the Mvskoke word, vnokeckv?

In this current political climate, the individual, or the artist, is looked upon with suspicion. If you don't fit squarely into "Christian," "family," or any other certified "safe" category (that is, not white, not identifiably male, female, married, straight, and so on) then you are in danger and you can be subject to great scrutiny and judgment. As I reread what I have written I ask myself if I have exaggerated, but I don't believe I have—suspicion and fear have grown in direct correspondence with the atrocities and human-rights violations inflicted by those in apparent power in the government, a government hand-in-hand with Christian fundamentalists. I am often in Oklahoma, my birthplace, for family and tribal events. I have noticed a definite spike in the climate of fear, marked by fundamentalist Christians who believe their way is the only way, by God. They've always believed this way but are increasingly self-righteous and secure in their power.

So how do we engender compassion in the middle of all this? Compassion doesn't depend on the reaction or response of others. It is, in its own right. I believe compassion gives the most overarching vision. Then, everything can fit, somehow. I'm trying to figure it out like everyone else. Art is a way to contribute to the figuring out. The artist bears witness, and can bring fresh vision into the world through art, to regenerate culture, to demand an accounting. I think of the recent exhibition at the Honolulu Academy of Arts by Hawaiian artist Kaili Chun. Her installation *Nau Ka Wae*, or *The Choice Belongs to You*, was a groundbreaking and award-winning meditation on compassion—native stones, which are living and considered to have their own voices in Hawai'i (and other native traditions) and appeared in the installation as a sort of consciousness.

You migrate back and forth between New Mexico and Hawai'i. As residences and as havens, what does each mean to you? Is there sustenance or power in the migration itself?
There has to be power or sustenance in migration or the world would be without humans, most plants, and animals. I have to find meaning in whatever I do—or even make meaning of meaninglessness. Not everything fits. Most things or ideas in this place don't fit seamlessly. Both New Mexico and Hawai'i were and are havens for me. I fled Oklahoma as a teenager. New Mexico gave me back my voice and continues to provide ongoing vision. My great-aunt Lois Harjo, whom I was especially close to, also spent much time there as a painter, inspired by the New Mexico Indian art scene. I followed behind her in this, and in my love for the arts. Hawai'i has given me the gift of water and I am continually inspired and challenged by the spirit of the Hawaiian people and land. We are painfully witnessing the destruction of this paradise. Actually, the Hawaiians and Mvskoke people are related. We each have stories that link us with each other.

You have stated that as an American Indian it is your responsibility— and indeed any American Indian's responsibility—to "pass on culture and to pass on hope." You have also noted that your primary audience is Indian country. Yet you also have a large non-Native following. Have you found resistance to you or your work from other American Indians because of its wide readership beyond those in Indian country? Alternatively, does resistance come from non-Natives because of your origins or your primary audience? If so, how do you respond—or is a response appropriate?
My audience crosses over. There is always resistance to anyone who is out there doing anything that crosses boundaries: of genre, culture, country, language, etc. That's just how it is. And there are always those who embrace you. I trust the work will find its way, just as I have to trust the process. Most of the resistance has come from those who find me not Indian enough . . . or too Indian. Or those who dislike women who speak out. Or those who find anyone carrying a

saxophone and dirtying the precious water of verse dangerous. Is any response necessary?

Have you had the opportunity to perform or work with native peoples in other regions—Central or South America, for example? Is there an increasing global context to the preservation of indigenous peoples and places—manifested either in literature and music and other arts, or in other contexts altogether?

Last year I performed in Argentina. That experience was mixed, except for the meeting with native people in the village of Amaicha. There were so many points of connection. The village was a mirror of an Isleta or Laguna village. The people looked the same, as did their houses and art. I felt I was in the houses of relatives of my Pueblo friends of the north. I also went to Cusco, and what emerged there was knowledge that this area was a navel for many tribal nations who migrated north. I saw the connection between Pueblos and the Mvskoke people. It is ancient.

At the Association of Writers and Writing Programs Austin conference's Joy Harjo tribute in March 2006, you read poetry, played saxophone, chanted, and sang. Do you have a favorite "genre" of performance? Reading/singing against live music, as with Poetic Justice, for example? Or, like much of your work, is the total of these performance types together greater than the sum of their individual parts? Do you envision incorporating filmed scenes into your live performances, given your filmmaking experience, as well?

I prefer a live band behind me. (And again, for the record, I no longer perform with Poetic Justice, though I might revive the name again for my new configuration.) There's also something fulfilling in the solo, naked voice performance. Yes, actually, I'm working on intersecting film and image with music and performance . . . right now.

You have maintained a blog for three years now—a fairly long time for the medium. What made you decide to start blogging, and is the impetus the same three years later? Has your other writing, or who you read, changed because of your blog? Do you sense any change in

literature overall because of blogging, or perhaps rather because of the
expansion of the Internet in general?

I have kept an ongoing journal over the years. The blog is an expansion
of it—with some editing. I don't know that my writing has changed
because of it—it's what I've always done. The difference is that I am
more aware of an audience, of readers—overall there's an expanded
awareness of the global. Before I went to school my world was vast
because I lived for the most part in my imagination. It was a live thing,
with as much texture and viability as what is called "real." My spirit
traveled all over the world. Songs and stories happened in the home,
via humans, and sometimes books. Then my world became the school
classroom and the discipline and rules, the path from the school to my
home, then after that a job, or a family. Anything that happened any-
where else happened in books, and sometimes in the news. My imagi-
nation then was bound in books, in reading. Then movies ushered in
the next level of reality, of expressive art. Videos followed. Then com-
puters and the Internet, which came with an expanded awareness of
the global. And with all this: less reading, fewer readers. Is this attrib-
utable to the Internet? Or, to the lack of ability to hear or believe the
spoken voice? Or to engage the human voice and person intimately?

What's next, Joy Harjo?

More poetry, more music, a book of stories, performance—and some
wisdom, knowledge, and peace for all of us.

Simmons B. Buntin is the founding editor of *Terrain.org: A Journal of the Built & Natural Environ-*
ments, at www.terrain.org. He is the author of two books of poetry: *Bloom* (Salmon Poetry, 2010)
and *Riverfall* (Salmon Poetry, 2005). He lives with his wife and two daughters in Tucson, Arizona,
but you may catch up with him online at www.simmonsbuntin.com.

The Thirst for Artistic Brilliance

[Interview with Pam Kingsbury, February 2003]

Where did you grow up? At what age did you know that you wanted to be an writer/artist/musician?
I grew up in Tulsa, Oklahoma. I knew from the beginning that I wanted to be an artist. My first urges were to draw and sing. My grandmother Naomi Harjo was a painter and we had her paintings in our house. I found great refuge in the act of drawing—to move into that creative space engaged my spirit in a way nothing else did at that very young age. I got in trouble for decorating the walls of the garage with chalk drawings. I also covered the closet of the kid's bedroom with my art. My mother was the singer, so we had music and her voice often holding our home together. I loved listening, and loved singing—privately. When other girl children my age were making plans to be teachers, nurses and brides (yes, brides)—I was always the only one who wanted to be an artist.

You have family connections in Alabama.
Yes, I have family connections in Alabama. My great-great (and between two and three more greats) grandfather was Menawa, or Monahwee as we spell it in Oklahoma. He and the Redsticks fought Andrew Jackson at the Battle of Horseshoe Bend. He was later removed to Oklahoma, despite his attempts to keep his people in their homelands in what is now known as Alabama and Georgia. My cousin George Coser, Jr. says he's buried near Eufaula, Oklahoma, but recently I received an e-mail from someone from Alabama, I believe, claiming descendancy, who says Monahwee was buried in Kansas. Monahwee's story is a story I wish to pursue for a full-length feature

film . . . . This whole western hemisphere is Indian country. There are amazing stories that form our history, but so much has been told by those who flatten and stereotype anything Indian. Often those who stereotype are our own people.

Let's talk about your time at the Institute of American Indian Arts (IAIA), the University of New Mexico (UNM), and the Iowa Writer's Workshop. How did you feel about the workshop? Have your feelings changed with distance?

This question could be a book. In fact, some of it will be. I'm currently working on a book of stories and many take place in those Indian school years, which was a time of great creative inspiration married with great despair. IAIA was an Indian boarding school run by the Bureau of Indian Affairs. In 1967 IAIA was a high school with a couple of years of postgraduate study. Students came from all over the United States—from Alaska, New York, Florida, everywhere. Many of us were from Oklahoma. We were all art majors from many different disciplines. I was there because of my artwork and at that time (my mother reminded me recently) I was drawing fashions. I had forgotten. She remembers that many of my designs later appeared in the fashion world. I had tapped into something. Later I became a drama and dance major and toured with one of the first all Native drama and dance troupes. I was one of the leads. This was a time of a tremendous awareness of change for Native peoples. We questioned . . . came to the conclusion that our cultural knowledge and exploration and creativity was our strength, and eventually I came to the conclusion, as did many others, that the wars within ourselves—whatever their source: colonization, the pressure of acculturation, and the ensuing family problems—were our ultimate strength, made us allies.

To be accepted into the Iowa Writers Workshop was quite a coup, and I went because it was considered the best writers workshop in the country. I had applied to four graduate programs and all of them except Iowa had offered me some kind of assistance, including graduate assistantships, scholarships. I basically drove into Iowa City with two children and all that we owned in the back of a small Japanese-made truck, and the promise of some assistance from the educational opportunity programs. We knew no one, and there was no visible

Indian community. I was torn away from the familiar and in a vulnerable position so I'm sure that set my lens. The first workshop the fall of 1976 was with a very well-known poet whose work I now admire. Then I didn't know her poetry; my catalogue of knowledge consisted nearly entirely of western U.S., non-European American, African, and Latin American poets. At UNM I was within eight hours of a BFA degree in Studio Art, painting and drawing. The poetry thing came later. Because of that Iowa poet/professor I considered quitting, walking away from the Iowa Writer's Workshop in the first month, and so did Sandra Cisneros, a Mexican-American poet from Chicago. I was the only Indian. Every week a worksheet of poems appeared in the English Department for each poetry workshop. The poems on the sheet were chosen from submissions from the respective classes. After nearly a month Sandra and I realized that neither of us had poems appear on the worksheet; we were the only ones in our class whose work had been ignored. We decided to approach the poet teaching our workshop together. We walked that sacred hall to her office, our sense of injustice making us brave. We knocked and stood at the door. At our appearance she flinched and made ready to run. We backed out. The next week we had work on the worksheets.

It became immediately obvious that I spoke a very different language, arrived in Iowa from a sensibility that was tribal, western, female, and intuitive, a sensibility different than most of the other workshop participants. I envied their excellent educations, their long study of poetry, their confidence in their knowledge, their art. There was no place to comfortably fit in a literary canon that was male and white. For sustenance several of us organized a Third World Writing Workshop. It included Sandra Cisneros; Kambone Obayani, an African-American novelist and horn player; Pam Durban, a southern woman writer; and Ricardo Longoria from south Texas, who was the only workshop participant who wasn't in the writing workshop. He was a graduate student in the rhetoric program of the English Department. I also occasionally took part in a feminist writing workshop at the university's women's center. Other workshop students and faculty were inspiration and support, including Dennis Mathis, a brilliant fiction writer and painter, Jayne Anne Phillips, also in fiction, and Rosalyn Drexler a playwright, painter, and novelist from New York who was once a visiting writer in the fiction program. I also spent most of my time the first year with the writers who were part of the International Writing Program. They included Leon Agusta, a poet from Indonesia, and Danarto, a playwright also from Indonesia. Being with them felt like home. The workshop atmosphere was a struggle as I felt a stranger there. Later I compared notes with those who felt so much at the center of the program, were outspoken, lauded. I was surprised that they too expressed similar sentiments. We were all there to be writers and the workshop was a crucible, a shop to forge writers for a competitive writing world. We were linked in that struggle, that thirst for knowledge, for artistic brilliance . . . . The last semester of my two years there four of us were chosen to read our work to possible private funders for the workshop program. There were two men and two women students, evenly divided between poetry and fiction. Jack Leggett introduced the writing program and then the student readers. I distinctly remember him emphasize that the program was primarily for male writers. I am often asked by my writing students and by young writers around the country regarding my experience at Iowa because they are interested in attending. I always tell them that the workshop was a useful technical school, probably the best. I had to nourish my soul otherwise.

Who are the writers who have influenced you?
I would have to begin with singers first who drew attention to lyrics bound to music. They are Patsy Cline, Billie Holiday, and Nat King Cole. Also Bob Dylan, John Coltrane, Miles Davis, and Jim Pepper. When I began writing it was first Simon Ortiz, the Acoma Pueblo poet, then Pablo Neruda, the Chilean poet, Leslie Silko, June Jordan, Adrienne Rich, especially Audre Lorde, and some African writers, including Okot b'Pitek and Amos Tutuola. Also, Galway Kinnell. His *The Book of Nightmares* is brilliant and necessary. There are many others, too.

How do you define yourself as a writer?
I take that to mean, am I of a particular school, a particular persuasion? I am most often defined by others as: Native American, feminist, western, southwestern, primarily. I define myself as a human writer,

poet and musician, a Mvskoke writer (etc.)—and I'm most definitely of the west, southwest, Oklahoma, and now my path includes Los Angeles and Honolulu . . . it throws the definition, skews it. It would be easier to be seen, I believe, if I fit into an easy category, as in for instance: The New York School, the Black Mountain School, the Beats—or even as in more recently, the slam poets. But I don't—

Do you have any particular discipline/writing routine?
It's often difficult, given my erratic schedule. When I am on a deadline schedule I write in the morning, which will often lead into the afternoon. Otherwise it's usually morning, before the logical mind takes control, and then I work on music in the afternoon. The music usually has to wait because a saxophone is loud and everywhere I've lived has assured me a live audience—so I practice music in the afternoon, when most people are at work. Here in Honolulu I live on a slope that is dense with houses—sound travels. If I am too late getting to sax practice I assume that I am giving a concert, and will often pull out jazz standards and play a dinner show! The birds like it. And sometimes the neighbors clap. All this to say, that discipline is important. I believe Colette said: "Discipline is the key to freedom."

Talk about your publishing experiences—you've published chapbooks with small presses as well as an anthology with a major press. . . . What are you currently working on? Do you have books in the pipeline?
My last three books were with Norton, a major publisher. My first book, *The Last Song,* was a chapbook from Puerto Del Sol Press; the next two, *What Moon Drove Me to This?* and *She Had Some Horses,* were published by independent presses respectively, I. Reed Books (Ishmael Reed and Steve Cannon's imprint, no longer viable) and Thunder's Mouth Books (now a subsidiary of Avalon Books). The next two were issued from university presses: *Secrets From the Center of the World,* the University of Arizona Press, and *In Mad Love and War,* Wesleyan University Press. I've been lucky as all the publishers, from *She Had Some Horses* on, have kept the books in print. I did try to first publish both *Horses* and *Mad Love* with Norton but both were rejected, rather eloquently. The third manuscript I sent them, *The Woman Who Fell from the Sky,* was accepted. I have been publishing

with them ever since. *How We Became Human, New and Selected Poems* was published in July 2002. A book of stories is forthcoming. I am also working on two new CD projects.

How does teaching influence writing?

I've taught intermittently since I graduated from Iowa. My first position was as an instructor at the Institute of American Indian Arts, which was a two-year fine arts school. Its first incarnation was as a Bureau of Indian Affairs boarding school turned into a fine arts high school, and is where I obtained my high school degree. Later I did a few stints as adjunct, then positions at the University of Colorado, Boulder, and the University of Arizona, where I was tenured. Next I was a full tenured professor at the University of New Mexico, then left teaching for about six years. I wanted to concentrate on my music, and managed to make a living performing and writing. Winter quarter of 1998 I was a visiting writer at the University of California at Los Angeles and then I taught again at UCLA this most recent fall and spring quarter, as a visiting professor in American Indian Studies and English. Teaching can feed the writing; it can also be detrimental. What feeds me is the research for each class, each course and the interaction with students. Discipline and intuition walk together and can even engender flight. Detriment can occur with department and university-wide politics, with large classes and huge numbers of pages to read, with balancing the needs of teaching with your own work. Most of us who are teaching artists are always in the middle of creative projects, which is why we are hired in the first place.

The fall quarter begins in a few weeks. I just picked out the students for my workshop, based on their submitted manuscripts. Because the set of a boxed book with CD I wanted is not available and I didn't find out until last week I will now have to rethink the syllabus—actually, I think it will work out better. Having read the students' poems I can better surmise what each one needs, the poets' work that will challenge, resonate for each one . . . . In my workshops I stress the importance of reading and studying poetry, as well as the need for the practice of the art. Half the workshop is in discussion of the assigned readings, the other half discussion of students' own poetry. Technical development is crucial but isn't everything. If there's no soul, there's no poetry . . . .

Talk about making the move from writing into music.
Poetry and music belong together—they came into the world together, they will leave together. If you want to get technical, then dance belongs as part of the equation. Every culture has a traditional base configured of poetry-music-dance, some of it secular, much of it sacred. Mvskoke philosophy can be gleaned from that base of such expression, as can Greek, other European, African, all cultures—at the Iowa Workshop the prevailing rule was that to embellish a poem or poetry with emotive expression was to tarnish the expression of it, to get in the way of the words. This has metamorphosed into the text-without-human-connection mode of thinking about poetry, about the making of literature. It must be a lonely world, that world.

Adding saxophone is another thing—and I took up saxophone in my very late thirties. Like writing it's a demanding discipline. Demands practice, study, and more practice. And faith, maybe faith is the prevalent force. Maybe faith also demands practice. And a love for the music, for the poetry, for the complexity of this strange and terrible place. In 1989 I started with Keith Stoutenburg in Tucson. We put together a little combo. He was on guitar, keyboard and voice, I played horn and spoke. We used the poems as a jumping off place. Later I hooked up with Susan Williams; we brought in Zimbabwe Nkenya to play bass. Zimbabwe is a way out, on-the-edge outside jazz player. With him we performed the first version of *Anna Mae* for a National Public Radio program. Then Susan's brother John moved to Albuquerque and we began Poetic Justice. Sometimes we'd work the music around the poems. Other times I'd bend the poems around the music, rewrite, add choruses, or a bridge. Since then I've written poems to go with particular vamps or melodies. Since, too, I've started another band, tentatively called, The Real Revolution.

What books do you recommend for young/novice writers?
I recommend that they read and hear poetry, from contemporary back through ancient times. That they listen to poetry, too, the poetry read from books, poetry performed, poetry that never finds its way in books. Most literature of the world isn't in books.

What books do you recommend for readers who may be unfamiliar with Native American writers/writing?
Where do I start? For fiction there's Leslie Silko, everything from her stories in the collection *Storyteller to Ceremony* to her latest, *Garden in the Dunes*; Greg Sarris, *Grand Avenue* and *Watermelon Nights*, James Welch's novels; Louise Erdrich, especially *Love Medicine* and her most recent novel, and there are more that I will wish had come to me on this late Monday afternoon . . . . For poetry, one of my favorite poets is Ray Young Bear, a Meskwaki poet; Simon Ortiz; there's Sherman Alexie who is a good poet; I like Elizabeth Cook-Lynn's most recent book of poetry—that's a start. Roberta Whiteman is excellent, too.

Where do you see your career in ten years? Twenty years?
I feel like I'm just beginning to find my way to my best work. It's about process.

You've written "poetry is synonymous with truth telling." Would you care to elaborate?
The artists: the poets, musicians, painters, dancers make art from truth. Art that forges new paths, new insight, inspiration, comes from the raw stuff floating in the connections between humans, animals, plants, stars, all life. Poets are the talk-singers, we find our art in the space between the words. There is where the truth lies. I also consider the African griots, those whose poetry is shaped particularly to tell the truth, whatever the cost.

You've been described as a mystic . . . .
The poet, too, can be a mystic, and I consider a mystic as one who sees beyond the obvious world, and moves accordingly. That is where my poetry has taken me and continues to lead me.

What do you believe/feel/know lies at the heart of your body of work?
Compassion. Joy.

Pam Kingsbury, author of *Inner Visions, Inner Views*, teaches at the University of North Alabama. A member of the National Book Critics Circle, her work has appeared in *Stand* magazine, *Library Journal*, *ForeWord* magazine, *First Draft*, and *The Encyclopedia of Alabama*.

In the Horizon of Light with Joy Harjo

[Interview with Ruben Quesada, August 2008]

Your contributions as an artist, activist, and feminist make you a role model for many writers, activists, and women. I'd like to know what drove you to become an activist and how do you feel about being viewed as a role model for being outspoken?
What I carry in my heart, my feet, are my mother's singing and my father's family's warrior ancestors who fought for justice. They have come together in my generation, in my time. I serve those gifts, or try to—along with others in my family, with my people, whose names you won't recognize.

Adrienne Rich has said about you that "she's generous in her poetry, opening her sacred spaces and music to all, yet never naive or forgetful about hostility and hatred." Your generosity and openness has allowed a mythical, meditative, and spiritual quality to resonate in your work. How do you feel this helps to distinguish your work from minority literatures and mainstream Anglo-American literary traditions?
The voice is the instrument of the spirit. I've had to follow it, and practice dutifully so I can attempt to translate all the valleys and mountains of it beautifully. Sometimes it speaks in poetry, other times via saxophone or singing. It's the same voice.

Concerning feminism, you've stated it "doesn't carry over to the tribal world, but a concept mirroring a similar meaning would." And "many women's groups have a majority of white women and [you] honestly can feel uncomfortable, or even voiceless sometimes." Has your senti-

ment changed since you made that statement or has there been any significant event(s), which have made you feel empowered or heard? My answer was inept and small. A major part of my struggle is directly related to being female in a society that disrespects or devalues female power. There is no balance of power in this society, this "over-culture." Not in government, not in the home. Not in public or private space. The predominant Christian religions include no female power in the power structure. How could there be life in this place without both? Common sense will tell you that it isn't possible!

We see the effects of this faulty operating system at all levels of society. The feminist movement inspired great change even though the larger community of predominately white feminists is different than say a small tribal community in Oklahoma. When I compare my mother's life, her inability to move freely in a life that could include her children, her home, and her music, to my life and the lives of my daughter and granddaughters, I see more openings, more movement. Some things have changed, some not at all. We're still grappling with a system in which anything related particularly to female experience is devalued, like teaching, childcare, or caretaking. The worst insult a boy or man can call each other is still: "woman," "girl," or "pussy." This wouldn't even be able to be constructed as insult in cultures in which the female experience and contributions are valued. Yes, there are hard realities of being a female sax player, for instance, in a field dominated by men, that can or might come into play when walking into a music store or talking to a sound man, or performing. I've had to focus on where I'm going, and keep going.

Would you say there is a tendency in contemporary American writing to exploit minority cultures for the sake of establishing American writing as a collection of diversity and culture in securing an ancestry, or do you see minority literature still struggling to be heard?
It's curious how powerful cultures of peoples have become "minority" in the vernacular. It's a power trick. The western hemisphere is Indian country and extends from the North Pole all the way to Tierra del Fuego and into the Pacific and Caribbean and within it are diverse and accomplished literary traditions. What is African also extends

throughout the Americas, to the continent of Africa and beyond and encompasses major literary traditions. And so on. How easily we are reduced to becoming once again dirty natives scrabbling for a voice. And yet if we are viewed through a slim, western perspective that travels back through Descartes and Christianity, all the way back, we will never add up to much. Try analyzing the Navajo Blessingway with western literary critical means. It's like measuring water with a measuring stick instead of a cup. I've challenged some of my Navajo writer friends to apply Navajo literary theory to Shakespeare, for instance. You'll get a very different reading. Yet, common sense theory tells you that both Navajo master texts and British master texts both have value.

Yes, we're still struggling to have a place here, though, ironically, we have a place. It's the fearful ones who try and keep us out who are still looking for a place.

You are a woman with many stories to tell about your experiences and the voice of your poems gives your readers some insight into who you are and where you've been. How has poetry helped you deal with the voices that make you who you are today?
Poetry became the voice of my spirit, a spirit that is much larger than all of my human failings. It's always teaching me something.

You are a "warrior" for many women and writers, and your love for the world around you comes through in your work. What advice do you have for minority writers who are fighting to be heard or who are struggling for legitimacy in American literature?
Remember that you are born with gifts that need to planted and grown. This "American" culture is young and rootless. It is adolescent with an adolescent sense of time and place that is "here and now," with no reference or power rooted in the earth, ancestors, or historical and mythical sense. Value your community and what that has to offer and continue to reach out beyond what you know to grow fresh ideas, meetings between borders, new roots.

What's your favorite work to read when giving a reading? Why?
It depends. New work excites me so I'm up for performing it—though it's a tricky risk. Sometimes it works, sometimes it doesn't quite, yet. "Fear Song" is an old favorite. I like to sing it. I sing many of my pieces during a reading, and often add sax.

Can you tell me what you're working on now?
I'm working on some instrumental music, more words and music (with singing and speaking), a book of stories, and a little courage and compassion.

Ruben Quesada is a Ph.D. student at Texas Tech University. His poetry and translations have appeared in *Rattle, Stand* magazine, *Southern California Review,* and *Third Coast.* His awards include residencies at the Squaw Valley Community of Writers, Lambda Literary Foundation Retreat, the Vermont Studio Center, and the Santa Fe Art Institute.

Writing, Constructing the Next World

[Interview with Bill Nevins, August 2008]

Please tell us a bit about your current recording release, tour plans, and your hopes for your current projects.

The new release, *Winding Through the Milky Way*, will be officially on its way in September. This is the realization of what I was working through in *Native Joy for Real*. In *Native Joy* I was stretching out, finding unique ways to express a cross between the poetry, music, and more direct incorporation of indigenous forms and ideas. I threw everything in together. I was experimenting. I believe that the new album is a fruition of that beginning sowed in *Native Joy*. I had an excellent producer in Larry Mitchell. The tour plans are as usual, which is usually in and out. Many of the tunes are songs that are part of one of my new projects, a one-woman-show with a band: *Wings of Night Sky, Wings of Morning Light*. The first reading with a band happened last December in New York City at the Public Theater. The second at the culmination of a Native playwrights' workshop set up by Native Voices at the Autry, in Los Angeles, a few weeks ago. Native Voices is going to produce the play for a March/April 2009 run in Los Angeles.

You've successfully explored and mastered several genres: print poetry, spoken word, poetry with music, song and, very notably, pure music, especially with your highly praised and demanding sax playing. Where do you see the coexistence and synthesis of these approaches taking your art? Do you enjoy any of these forms more than others?

The play *Wings of Night Sky, Wings of Morning Light* is the place where all of this can come together. I have to think of all these forms as one expression and move towards a cohesive whole, or I'd go crazy!! I also photograph and wish to include those images in the setting.

Your new third original album takes up and advances the themes and musical ideas of Native Joy for Real, *your previous album. Would you comment on the process of bringing this album to completion and your hopes in the process?*
Each project has a spirit. *Native Joy for Real* came forth despite a traumatic injury. It doesn't look or sound quite like anything else, a kind of hybrid. This new album takes the various elements that are hanging loose and melds them. I remain inspired by Jim Pepper's crossovers, and I am moving ahead toward my own realizations and experiments. I want this album to communicate to listeners in a way that is beautiful and revolutionary.

Many listeners would say that you sing in at least three distinct voices in performance and on recordings—that of your sax and of course your own singing voice, as well as your spoken word poetry delivery. Do you consciously choose which voice to exercise for specific thoughts, emotions, effects?
I don't know that I consciously choose which. Singing was the first voice I employed. I love to sing, as did my mother, until around fourteen, when I was forbidden to sing in our home. I left it behind then. I see or hear them all as one voice.

You have said that you most prefer performing with a band. Would you comment on the evolution of your band sound and organization, especially recently? What is your current recording and touring band line up, and how did this come to be?
I like having company on stage. There are more possibilities. Solo is all right too. Both are different experiences. With a band I stay with the standard rock set up: guitar, keyboard, bass and drums. I do sometimes go out with just Larry and his guitar and his/our looped and looping sounds. My current set up is Larry Mitchell, the amazing guitar giant, Howard Cloud on bass, amazing, Robert Muller on keyboards, who intimidated me when I first heard him. They all did! I've learned much from them and continue to learn. For drums it's usually Steven Alva-

rez, on drums and Native voice, who also performs with Medicine Dreams, an Alaska band. Right now I call the band Joy Harjo and the Arrow Dynamics Band. It's not the right name, yet.

The recording was mostly just me and Larry, with Robert on some tunes, and another few voices in a couple of places.

Although the band Poetic Justice disbanded many years ago, still people commonly refer to your performances as Joy Harjo and Poetic Justice. Have you considered reviving the band name sometime in the future in response to this unfading (if incorrect) popular perception?
I've thought about it. I decided to let the name go because it was so associated with a cool, reggae jazz sound. I am trying to find another way to use the Poetic Justice name, with a change. Any ideas?

Do you see your work as political in some sense?
Everything is political, whether you choose to see it that way or not. I've weathered fierce tribal politics, canoe club politics, music, poetry, and everything has politics. With whatever you say or do you are making a stand, one way or the other. And even that you are saying or doing something makes a stand.

You travel often between your home in Hawai'i and your teaching work in New Mexico. The high desert and the ocean beaches—quite a notable geographic contrast! And of course you tour with readings and performances nationally and internationally. What role does travel and changing situations/places have in your artistic awareness and in your writing?
Some of us move more vertically in the world. We stay in one place and go deep. Others, like me, move more horizontally. We go out and bring back new ideas, synthesis, change.

Both New Mexico and Hawai'i can be described as "Indian Country" or "Native Country." Do you see a separate culture outside the "United States" culture? What about the crossing of borders and boundaries, politically and culturally?
I've always called the U.S. culture the "over-culture" and don't consider it a true culture. Beliefs, social institutions, arts, and traditions

construct culture. The United States is made up of many cultures. There is no such thing as a melting pot. There are various cultural streams that are renewed, slowed, cut off, or otherwise changed. The over-culture is a culture of buying and selling.

You teach creative writing at the University of New Mexico. What thoughts do you have for young and new writers coming up?
Those who write are assisting in constructing the next world, the next consciousness. Be open, aware, and study. Study with all parts of your being, not just your intellect. Some of your knowledge may come from books, most of it from other sources. Always allow yourself to be surprised. And, write.

What writers and recording artists interest you recently?
I am reading the Macquarie PEN Anthology of Aboriginal Literature out of Australia, edited by Anita Heiss and Peter Minter, the stories of Patricia Grace, a Maori writer, and poems by Bengali poets, especially Sunil Gangopadhyay. As for music, my listening is eclectic: everything these days from James Brown to Hawaiian traditional to Michael Brecker and Luis Miguel.

You'll be performing soon in Taos and in September in Albuquerque. Will these both be with your band, or solo shows? Any thoughts and hopes for these performances, which are being greatly looked forward to by your fans?
I have three performances lined up in New Mexico this late summer/ fall. It's nice they coincide with the album release. All three are band performances. And we'll have new CDs for sale (and the older ones!). New Mexico audiences are my heart and soul and I'm always happy to perform here.

Bill Nevins, based in Albuquerque, New Mexico, is a cultural journalist, poet, and educator. Nevins publishes regularly in *AbqARTS, Local iQ, Trend, Z Magazine, Roots World*, and other outlets. He teaches writing at the University of New Mexico, Valencia Campus, and is the UNM chapter president of the American Association of University Professors (AAUP).

Transcending Writing on Singing Wings

[Interview with Tanaya Winder, May 2010]

The transition between night and day seems to be of great importance in this play. Can you explain what you wanted that choice to emphasize and (perhaps) how that does or doesn't relate to the title, Wings of Night Sky, Wings of Morning Light, *you've chosen for your play?*
The day relates to the temporal world—to that above the surface. The night is mystery, that which is beyond the grid of logic. It's the transition, or the in-between state of twilight, the grey before dawn when we get the kind of insight we can drag into the being-ness of our lives. Mystery wears clothes. What is sacred is touchable. Most of the play happens at night. It is only when the Spirit Helper sings the Spirit Helper song, when the mother's spirit has departed after coming to visit her daughter Redbird that the possibility of sunrise occurs. The song follows a traditional song pattern. The order of the colors is ceremonial as we begin to see the emergence of sunrise. This makes a path for Redbird to enter back into the possibility of wholeness. And when Spirit Helper brings Redbird back to the kitchen table, after the car wreck, Redbird emerges in the light, and in the Mvskoke creation story being told by her grandmother: "The light made an opening in the darkness . . . ." "Wings" refer to flight, which can be escape, transcendence, the ability to see and know, or to perceive beyond earth gravity. And the need to balance is at the root of most Native ceremonies. The story of an individual is within the context of a larger family story. The balancing of an individual changes the family dynamic. For clarity and health, there must be a balance in the family, individual body and soul, or community system. The left and right, the earth and sky, dark and light, must be in coherent loops for vibration to make a clear resonance.

Let's talk about the kitchen table. I am reminded of your collection of poetry, The Woman Who Fell from the Sky; *the final poem of that collection is "Perhaps the World Ends Here" with the opening line, "The world begins at the kitchen table." After re-reading that poem in light of your play, I began to think of how much* Wings of Night Sky, Wings of Morning Light *really embodies that poem. Can you address this connection and whether or not that was a conscious choice?*

I had decided to write a one-woman show a few years before I actually got to it. The notion came often to me often during music performances or readings because when I perform I weave stories around the songs and poems. I began to envision a show with a definite trajectory, with drama and coherency between all the elements. I worked on it most of the summer of 2007 then gave up in frustration because I just couldn't find it, though I had piles of material to work from. I didn't have the central vehicle to unite the pieces. I was informed about the new Native Initiative at the Public Theater and told to contact the Menominee actor and director Sheila Tousey, because they were looking for plays. That was around late August/early September of 2007. I remember promising Sheila on the phone: "Yes, I can have a play written for a play reading by December," then hanging up wondering what I had gotten myself into, as I had never written a stage play. It's different from screenwriting, short stories or other storytelling forms. It was Betsy Richards, a program officer at the Ford Foundation, whose portfolio funded the Native Initiative, who reminded me that she always loved the kitchen table poem, and why not use the kitchen table as the central device. Once I had that, all the pieces I had wrestled with all summer came together.

I was really drawn to the space of the kitchen table—how you used it as a dinner table, a hiding place, a bar, the father's dead body, can you speak to the different manifestations of the kitchen table in the show?
The kitchen table used to be the heart of the house. I don't know if that's necessarily the case any more for many in this country. As I discovered the story, I discovered the agility of the kitchen table metaphor.

Did you feel a different energy come out of the kitchen table once it jumped from the page on to the stage?

The page and stage are similar in that they are dreaming spaces. Each has their own set of natural laws of aesthetics, form, and manners of movement. The page is flat and intimate. The action is internal. The stage is a large physical space, in a place with audience. The kitchen table on stage keeps a coherency, but the space around it changes every performance. The stage, and live performance overall, is one of the most immediate, creative spaces. It's live, so alive it can appear to be living and breathing on its own, when you are in the thick of it. The only control you have is over what you are carrying in your center, your memory and everything that has brought you to that moment. The page, however, has a more controllable environment. Every performance I interact with the table, the idea of the table, and how the story moves around it. It's never the same. It's always a different energy. Maybe it's the same way with reading. You, the reader, or audience are never quite the same.

There are some very strong images associated with voice and silence: "Watch out, we tried, but couldn't tell our mother. Our tongues were stuck with taffy in our mouths." Can you elaborate more on how you view sound and silence working in the play?
Silence is a space of creative possibility, even as it can be a space of shutting down. Every phenomenon in this realm has oppositional potential. The play begins with the silencing of Redbird by her stepfather, or "The Keeper" who takes her music, her voice away from her. The Keeper is invested in the invented story of America. He believes in the hierarchical value system laid down in the European Christian beginnings of the takeover of indigenous lands. In that scale of measure, an Indian woman and her children are not worth as much as a white male. They are seen as property. I am reminded of one of the essays in June Jordan's brilliant book of essays, *Civil Wars*. As she was divorcing, she discovered that there were more laws in the American system, for taking care of property rights, that is the couch, than the rights of her son. *Indigenous* people in this country have been disappeared in the story of America. For us to speak means we carry breath. Each of us, Native and non-Native, must deal with how this creates itself in us, as these lands are indigenous. The root story is indigenous. In a sense, we have become the anti-story of those who would disap-

pear us from the American story, and are therefore dangerous to them. That story is implied as the foundation of the play. Redbird's story was silenced by history and in her home. She was broken open in the car crash, so the story could emerge.

I know time and time again you've been asked about the relationship between music and poetry in your work and I absolutely love the power music holds in your play. I'm thinking of the Trail of Tears song where two women sing a song to hold each other up and how the mother character gives Redbird a song to save her. What role did you envision music having within the play?

I never considered writing the play without music. The stories and music emerged together. I don't always know exactly what or why I'm doing. The interweaving of stories, poetry, and music emerged organically as I traveled about to read. About fourteen years ago at a performance in Portland, Oregon, a young Crow man waited until all the audience had left to approach me. I could see that he was one of the "old" young people, and that he'd been raised by grandparents. He said my performance reminded him of the way he was taught, with story, poetry, and song woven together.

I appreciated the leaps in time your play took from reflecting on the main character's (Redbird's) beginnings, both historically and ancestrally, to focusing on the present and even future. I was fascinated by the grandfather who was capable of "bending time" and got the sense that this is what we, as artists, do, bend time? Do you consider yourself a bender of time, artistically?

I loved those stories of my actual great-(times seven) grandfather Monahwee who could bend time. I've used the bending time family gift for deadlines, and for traveling, in a small way. And have seen time as an actual being, shifting and moving. I have not been trained in the way Monahwee was, back in those times. (And people are still being trained in similar manners.) But yes, artistically, especially in poetry, I am aware of bending time. When I write I am always aware of eternal time as it comes up against present, linear time. I intently work to make an opening in consciousness with both strategies of time . . . even in story and music, but especially in poetry.

Spirit Helper reminds Redbird when her mother once again leaves her: "There are some things that take an eternity to understand." I believe we are present in eternity and present here, though present in each in a very different fashion. The mind of eternity cannot fit solidly in any word or story. But when we see the tail or breath of it, we know it, without question.

I enjoyed the participatory aspect of your play, the way Redbird often speaks to and even directly addresses the audience, such as when she begins by saying "Your good thoughts will help see us through." I felt it somehow gave the audience agency in what they were experiencing. Does being able to address your audience directly offer a different satisfaction from poetry where you don't always see your reader?
Being on stage as a character gives me a much different satisfaction. I am often speaking poetry, mixed with storytelling and music. Poetry is more compact, fills a quieter space. On stage, in character, I am aware of mystery from a different angle. When I read someone else's poetry, I hear the lone voice of the poet, which is almost never alone. I hear the voices behind the voice, which are sometimes ghosts, birds, lovers, ex-lovers, or the sound of shattering or putting back together.

I'm curious as to how it felt to work with so many mediums, acting, singing, and the music; are there any similarities between constructing a poem and a play? Or song?
There is a similarity with all of them, and that is, you start with the unseen and bring something into being. A poem is much more solo. It's your soul's ears listening to the sound of the collective soul. Your ears may be directed to a certain event, country, time, object, person, or emotional stream. Music often begins that way for me also—and the voice and the horn carry the melody, which is like the poetic line. The rest usually forms around it, though I have next often started with rhythm. I am a rhythm freak. Always tapping out, listening, responding to the various rhythms. I am a dancer at heart, and few people know this about me. I find images or sounds by moving them, and moving with them. Images may also be at the heart of a song. A play is more like writing a symphony and telling a story, at the same time, especially a play with music.

How did acting and the actual embodiment of words that, in terms of poetry, we only get to experience during readings affect your overall perspective on the craft of writing?

My first visceral step into poetry was watching a television show in the early seventies in which a tribal person in ceremony became the poem/ritual song that he was singing. You have to be exact so that what you embody is what you imagine. And in your exactness you have to leave a place for mystery, so that the unknowable has a way to enter. Acting is an extension of words. It is words made manifest by the body.

Are there any plays that have or playwrights who have influenced you?

. . . All of the children's plays we performed throughout elementary school. I was always in school plays though I was socially very shy. I was often picked because the teachers would say, "your voice carries." Of course there's Shakespeare. Shelagh Delaney's *A Taste of Honey*, about a young working class English girl who falls in love with a black sailor. It was very controversial when it premiered in the late fifties. I was on the crew for the play at Indian school and it was there I got pulled into performing in one of the first all Native drama and dance troupes. Monica Charles, a Klallum playwright was a postgraduate student at the Institute of American Indian Arts, when I was a high school student. I had a lead in her play *Mowitch*. We toured the Pacific Northwest with our performances, which included dance. Rolland Meinholtz, a Cherokee, was our beloved teacher. He taught us to be professionals. We performed one of his plays, *Black Butterflies*. I also think of Cherrie Moraga, August Wilson, Tennessee Williams, Ionesco, Euripides, and Lorraine Hansberry.

Finally, I recall a line "Spirit Helper told me, we have to return to the beginning of the story if we are to find all the pieces." I'm curious, what do you consider the beginning of your story and journey as an artist?

I consider the very beginning of it as unknowable. It started before "I" did. It started with my mother's longings to sing, her poetry-speech. It started with my father's ache to know, give voice to mystery when he saw so much racism and violence. And then before that, and before that . . . However, in "real" time . . . .it was the same way. As a child, the world felt anew with every unheard song made hearable, every unspoken poem made speakable. But, back to the linear here and now, before I was five I felt most myself while dancing, singing and making art. I knew it then.

Do you plan on writing more plays in the future?
My next play, which is bothering me like crazy right now, will also include music. The characters and music keep bothering me. The play is waking me up at night. I will be on it after I finish three other writing deadlines.

One line "There is power in this song," really stands out in my mind; I believe it is because there is definitely power in Wings of Night Sky, Wings of Morning Light. *Thank you so much for sharing this gift with us.*
And *mvto*, thank you, Tanaya.

Song Language

Creating from the Heart, Out

[Interview with Loriene Roy, winter 2009]

You're an accomplished writer of many forms—poetry, plays, music, short stories. Tell us about your journey to also write picture books. How do you approach writing picture books? Is this process different than the one you follow in your other writing?

I've written two picture books and the approach and impetus for each was different. *The Good Luck Cat* came about shortly after the birth of my first grandchild. It was with her birth that the need to tell stories was released in me. I wanted her to know about my beloved Aunt Lois Harjo, and the stories she told me. Aunt Lois told me that some cats are good luck, and there aren't many in this world. She also filled me in about belonging to the Katcv or Tiger Clan, so we have a relationship with cats. The book honors that connection with cats. The story came first. My intention was to write about a niece and nephew's cat who died, to help them come to terms with their grief, but the story took its own path and I followed it. When I contracted with Harcourt for the book they allowed me choose an artist. Harcourt contracted with him, a rare thing, I learned later, as publishers usually insist on their own choice of illustrator. When the artist didn't come through with finished art, after we waited for two years, they found illustrator Paul Lee, who created the final images for the story. And the book was finally published several years after the first rough draft of the story.

For a Girl Becoming was a poem written for a coming of age event honoring a grandchild. I mean it for all of my grandchildren. And, the wise ones remind us that all are our children. The editor, Patti

Hartmann at the University of Arizona Press, helped find Mercedes McDonald as illustrator. Mercedes and I worked together in conceptualizing the images for the story. We practically dreamed the images together. Her paintings make the book.

How does writing for young readers and their families impact your other writing?
I'm not quite sure how it does. Everything I do, from poetry, to prose, to children's books, music, and performing all make a continuum. I create from the heart, out, and am always looking towards forms of expression that will refresh the present and future shape of culture. I often meld forms to make a new one. The poem in *For a Girl Becoming* is ceremonial and relates back to various tribal traditions of acknowledgment of the coming of age of a child. That it's in English and in a book fits the time and reality of our current lives.

What were some of your favorite books as a child?
My favorite was the *Golden Books Family Treasury of Poetry*, selected and with commentary by Louis Untermeyer. I loved the Mrs. Piggle-Wiggle books. I loved *Island of Blue Dolphins*, *A Wrinkle in Time*, Charles Dickens novels, and just about anything else I could smuggle into my quiet reading place: the closet. Within a month of learning to read in first grade, I devoured everything with print. I was sent to the second grade classroom to read from their shelves.

What writers for young people are important to you?
Debra Frasier has been important and helpful to me. *On the Day You Were Born* was poetic, and spoke powerfully to many ages. She assisted in getting my first children's book published.

What new opportunities have arisen for you from writing picture books?
After performances I often have a selection of my books and CDs for sale. I enjoy signing and speaking with audience members. I have several different audiences and they sometimes don't cross over. The poetry audience doesn't always know I am a musician with a body of work, and vice versa. And neither is usually aware that I have written

a children's book (now two books), and seeing *The Good Luck Cat* for sale on the table surprises them. It's usually one of the first items to sell out. Picture books create a new audience. Important is that young Native students see themselves. When you are not seen, as happened to my generation, a generation taught to read by the Dick and Jane series, you are basically disappeared from the story realm of meaning informing your mainstream social world. It's also important for them to know it's possible for them to create their own stories.

How have readers responded to your first picture book, The Good Luck Cat?
I have heard many times over how much children love to hear the book. It's a most requested bedtime story, according to many who take the time to tell me. I often read the book in classrooms to young students. The students' hands shoot up immediately when I begin the story because they are moved to share. They ask about Woogie and everything that befalls Woogie. They want to share their own stories of their animal friends. As I've read it over the years I get more and more inventive with the performance of the reading. I enjoy it and so do the students. The book brings up many questions, questions of losing and finding, dreaming, violence, the love of animals, hunting, of the need for companionship by animal friends . . . .

You spend your time between New Mexico and Hawai'i and have lived in and visited many other places. How are these places special to you? How do they play a part in the setting of For a Girl Becoming?
We are a multicultural world. We have always been multicultural. My tribal nation was situated near the Mississippi, the Gulf coast, and the Atlantic. All kinds of influences washed through. People intermarried, exchanged stories and ideas. This has been going on since the world was created. Air travel has increased the opportunity for connections and sharing. And some are the ones in our family who are charged with gathering stories to infuse the consciousness with new matter. The poets, musicians, writers, and artists usually have that role. I left Oklahoma for New Mexico in high school to attend the Institute of American Indian Arts. (It was a high school with two years of a post-graduate curriculum in the late sixties.) I was blown open creatively

because all of us were young Native artists, from tribal nations from each corner of the United States. We inspired each other and were also inspired with mainstream social and cultural events. Though we were young, we were aware that our art had to bring forth that which defined us as tribal, as well as incorporate what inspired and fed us, like Coltrane, Jackson Pollack, and pop culture. I graduated from high school from IAIA and have lived most of my life in New Mexico. I continue to leave and return. I have recently returned again. I lived in Hawai'i for about eleven years. I don't know that Hawai'i plays an integral part in *For a Girl Becoming* but it has in my life. The ocean has taught me to trust the mysteries of the deep, and shown me how to navigate through changes of emotional weather. The Hawaiian culture has reminded me of the power of cultural expression to grow and hold a people together, no matter governance, or gun power. Song language is loved and respected there, so yes, Hawai'i is important to my newest book. There are several indigenous cultural threads and references in the book because my grandchildren are multicultural beings. The book references Mvskoke, Navajo predominantly, as well as Pueblo and Cherokee.

The baby's birth coincides with numerous blessings—with rain arriving from the Pacific, pollen blowing through the house, and hundreds of running horses. As the girl grows older, she continues to receive these blessings and in turn her life is recognized as a blessing and her task is to continue to bless. How do these thoughts reflect an indigenous view of the world, especially reciprocity?
We are all born within a familial stream of connection. It grows us and in turn we feed it. We live in give and take. That's basic human law, and many indigenous cultures still consciously practice it.

One feature of the baby's birth is song: the singing (and dancing) of medicinal plants. The singing also attracted which brought on the blessing of rain. What were these plants and their roles? How do they express the Native view of wellness as a balance in life?
Which plants depends on which geographical area the tribe lives in, or lived in originally. There are over five hundred indigenous nations and cultures, each with helpers. There are established relationships. Plants

are beings and require respect and singing if they are to be helpful. We all owe our lives to the helpfulness and sacrifice of plants. Corn is very powerful. Corn has managed to be included as an ingredient in almost every manufactured "food" item in this country. The impetus of corn therefore is very powerful. If we enslave plants, disrespect them, abuse them, we get the same in return. Look at tobacco, for instance. It is a beloved plant for my people, and is actually a different plant than used in the manufacture of tobacco products. We used to use it sparingly. It's a powerful plant. The power gets angry when misused. We are all familiar with the effects of excessive tobacco use: lung disease, strokes, and heart problems.

Native people recognize and celebrate both women's ways and men's ways. The baby in For a Girl Becoming *receives an inheritance in the form of specific gifts from her mother and father. Tell us about these gifts. Were they based on the gifts you received from your parents? Are these the gifts you have given your children and grandchildren?*
These are gifts particular to the child, from the two sets of grandparents, though most have been passed from one generation to another.

The baby in For a Girl Becoming *was welcomed with ceremony and a gathering of her relatives. How does this reflect ceremonies that families hold to welcome babies into their families?*
Children are considered the continuance of life. They are spirits who have come to share the world with us. We have a responsibility to nurture their gifts, to teach them. A ceremony or gathering cements the relationship and responsibilities. The over-culture has infantilized children and the experience of children. And the over-culture keeps us as children so we do not question consumption and the needs of our souls. (Over-culture is a term I created to name the false culture that traps us economically, whose products do not feed our souls with filling cultural song-story-art food.)

Houses play important roles in the story. Before the baby entered this world, she lived in a spirit house. Her mother's body may have been the rainbow house. She was born in a desert house. Her parents' gifts came from their houses of genealogy and personality. Her family hoped she would always have her home. Please explain the prominence of the house. How does this relate to Native views of belonging and connection to the land?

A house can be a home. Houses may assume importance here because my tribe was uprooted from our homelands East of the Mississippi River and forced to Indian Territory in what is now known as Oklahoma. Our homes were burned behind us, or taken over by colonizers. We are still recovering. This is true for many tribal peoples in this hemisphere. This process of takeover is still ongoing, in more recent years with the U.S. government's relocation program.

The girl in For a Girl Becoming *is given advice on protocol or cultural etiquette. She is told to share water, food, and kindness. Tell us about the role of protocol in the story.*

It is important that the child reading about and participating in the story understand that protocol means respect. It is respect for oneself, gifts, family, and everyone's place in the world. And the poem was written as a ritual act so protocol is really the bone structure.

You once wrote that "at the presence of birth I have always felt death standing nearby." How is this side of life also shown in For a Girl Becoming*?*

I don't directly show this in *For a Girl Becoming*, but I do acknowledge the tests and dangers that each of us faces in our lives.

In your short story, "The Reckoning," your mother calls you a dreamer. What is the role of dreaming in For a Girl Becoming*?*

First of all, it isn't my mother calling me a dreamer. The story "The Reckoning" is somewhat autobiographical fiction. The mother is fictional as is much of the story. Dreaming could be the same thing as imagination. Everything is imagination. We are imagining ourselves. This computer I am typing on is solidified imagination. Each of our paths is born of the imagination of our ancestors and our own personal spirit.

You once said, "My work is woman identified." Do you think of your-self as a writer for girls? Do you also see yourself writing a picture book that might be called "For a Boy Becoming"?

You're ahead of me! I'm already planning for the book "For a Boy Becoming." I have two grandsons who will be coming of age. One is eight and one is ten. The book is percolating.

Can you tell us about the illustrations in For a Girl Becoming? *How do you think the artist depicted Native influence in the illustrations without veering toward stereotypical imagery?*

I have nothing but praise for Mercedes McDonald. She is a sensitive and powerful image-maker. Mercedes's illustrations are beautiful and unique and not stereotypical. It's always been important to me that we Native people are seen as human beings. The public tends towards Native images and illustrations that continue to present us in tradi-tional dress and in mythic situations and stories. These have a place, but this shouldn't be the only context in which we are seen. I want my grandchildren to be able to see themselves. I want all children to be able to see themselves in each other. I want anything I am involved in to help us reimagine ourselves as beautiful and powerful, all of us.

Finally, what's next for you as far as future writing projects?

For a Boy Becoming, of course. I'm in the midst of a "memoir," a book of poetry, and also working on music and a play.

Congratulations on the beauty and poetry of For a Girl Becoming. *I look forward to suggesting it to librarians, parents, and young readers.*

Loriene Roy was born and raised in rural towns bordering the Fond du Lac Reservation in northern Minnesota. She is Anishinabe, a member of the Minnesota Chippewa Tribe, and is enrolled on the White Earth Reservation. Roy received a master's degree in library science from the University of Arizona and a Ph.D. from the University of Illinois at Urbana-Champaign. She is a professor in the School of Information at the University of Texas at Austin, where she teaches graduate courses in reference, public librarianship, reader's advisory, and library instruction / information literacy.

You Might as Well Dance

[Interview with Harbour Winn, Elaine Smokewood, and John McBryde, summer 2009]

Joy, when I read your poetry I'm aware that dancing and movement seem so important to you. What do you experience when you're dancing? How does this image of dancing run through your words?
For me, dancing has always meant the ability to move about in the world without question. I was often the shyest person and the quietest person until I got on the dance floor. Those who thought they knew me would question: Who was that? Dancing was the one thing I could do and be absolutely myself without any restrictions. I've found a similar movement in the writing of poetry. I have found it in music. Writing poetry is a way of moving. How dancing works through all of my poetry, I'm not sure exactly, but I know it's there. One of my best earlier poems is "There Was a Dance, Sweetheart," in *What Moon Drove Me to This?* The whole poem was an awareness of dance, of the dance of life, of the dance of a particular relationship or movement from a meeting to a departure, from a sunrise to a sunset. We can either be dragged by circumstance or we find a way to dance. In a piece in *A Map to the Next World* I was reminded by my muse that if you're going through hell, you might as well dance.

Following up on Harbour's question, I was thinking about the poem "The Evening Song," and how that it ends on the word "bury." Bury is usually an ending kind of word, but in the rhythm of that poem it's like the poem doesn't end. We have an ending and a word that's strongly associated with ending, but the rhythm of what's happening at the ending of that poem isn't really letting the poem end. So often in

your poetry I feel like I'm entering into a poem that really doesn't have a beginning or an ending. Is that something that you think about?
I still haven't really worn that poem; it's fairly new. Maybe in that particular poem it's related to moving through water and I'm moving through in an outrigger canoe, moving through grief, a small bit of grief. Water is movement. Usually, you go back on earth to bury. On an island you take to the ocean for burying and healing. And yes, I think there's something to your statement, I feel that often the poems aren't so declarative in time and space. They are part of a larger narrative, lyric or song. What we see on the page, or hear in the air is just the earthly part of it. I am always aware of different kinds of time, every moment of past, present, future. Poems are often lenses to see into time, they aren't always confined by the page, by air.

I feel sometimes like a poem was kind of there, like something preceded this poem and something goes on after it. And this little piece is just part of something bigger that doesn't have an ending or a beginning; it's kind of confined on the page, which is really exciting and wonderful.
Yeah, maybe that's what's happened. That's a newer poem and in some of the older more prosaic poems, I may have overwritten. I read the long narrative poem "Wolf Warrior" the other day, for the first time in a few years As I read I realized that probably two thirds of it needs to be cut. Maybe this trimming need is part of a larger trend that's come about from working on music, as I turn poems to lyrics, and sifting down to what's most important. I have a tendency to over-analyze, and realize that I often indulged myself in some of those longer, denser narrative pieces.

Last night you said that you don't have any illusions that the poem comes from you. I really like that. My own experience with creative things is I just got lucky and was there when it arrived. Can you elaborate on that some?
Yeah, I've had students who ask "if that's true, then do you just go write when you get inspired?" and I tell them you can't do that. If you just write when you're inspired, you may never write. You have to sit

there and be open, ready, even as you are writing to discover. Sometimes nothing will happen or will appear to happen. But I've learned that something is always happening. Then maybe months later what I thought wasn't happening suddenly appears as a gift. I realize that there were roots to that poem or story or song that go back before all the meandering around. But as to where they come from, who knows? Sometimes I feel like I'm just constructing little houses for the poems or for the songs, I'm making a place for them, and if they like it, if they think it looks nice enough or they like the feel of it, a spirit will move into it and live there.

In talking about this place from which the voices come, don't you sometimes write about tricksters, lots of times, maybe? When you're in that place where voices come, are there tricksters that confound and fool you, too?
Oh, yeah. I think tricksters always have two sides to them. There's a purpose to tricksters and sometimes they're like laughter and crying all rolled into one, and they can startlingly open something up just as they can slam something shut. There's always that duality to them. In our tribe, the Muskogee tribe, trickster is rabbit. I always remember Bob Thomas, the Cherokee culturalist and storyteller extraordinaire, telling me, "The rabbit's not male or female, it's both. It's always walking that line between the sacred and the profane—the trickster is always about the duality between here and there, sun and moon, sky and earth. Somebody has to patrol, I suppose, or be on that line making sense of what really can't be made sense of. Sometimes I think what I do as a poet or as a human being is walk that line. And when you walk that line and you listen and you watch, you meet the other tricky ones. And even as you think you might be fooling them, they fool you. I don't think there's anybody on earth who's not beyond being fooled, or we wouldn't be here. This is earth. But everybody, everything serves a purpose, and tricksters serve that purpose of embodying the sublime and the ridiculous.

I think I'm raising a topic to hear your wonder within. One of your earlier poems reminds me of what you're talking about now. There's

a line in "I Am a Dangerous Woman" that made me look back at the
date it was published, for it seems like a post–9/11 poem, but it's not.
There's a line about weapons that security systems will never detect
and about which guns can or even should always click in your head.
Security will never find these; of course, security has changed these
days. We're more insecure than ever, now one of the most despised
countries in the world, thanks to our "security" problem. The meaning
of the word "security" has acquired other nuances of meaning, heavy
baggage from these times. That was one of my earliest poems, when I
lived in fog and it was only poetry that would focus my psyche in the
present-time field. Of course I wouldn't write the same poem now. I
don't know about "wonder within"—there is no edge to wonder.

I was really struck last night hearing you speak, for I thought you
were one of the few public speakers that I have heard in my life who
was the least negative and the least judgmental and the kindest. You
were so careful in everything you said, never talking about them with-
out including yourself among them. You did not talk about your own
ways of doing things as if they were some kind of universal law. I
admired that so much. And I'm thinking it was not an accident that
she's presenting herself this way. What kind of energy do you see your-
self putting out when you're on a stage speaking or performing? Do
you feel that you live by that kind of non-judgmental-ness, that you're
putting that positive energy out there?
We're all putting energy out whatever we're doing . . . we're in a con-
stant stream of energy, and we're either singing or making noise.
Sometimes a little wisdom breaks through, other times (as you can see
by the chaos of this spoken draft of the interview!), it doesn't. I ask
for help. I asked for help last night, as it can take awhile for yourself
to catch up to yourself. I lean towards compassion but I struggle like
everyone else with all my human complications. There's an onomato-
poeic word in Hawaiian, li'ili'i, which means "small," as in small-
acting. That self is quite energetic and likes to get its way. Last night I
wasn't up to it . . . the compassionate self stepped forward. It always
reminds me that I'm serving poetry, the source of poetry. It's much
larger than me, than the li'ili'i self.

Incredibly wise and mature.

So I've learned a lot along the way. That's why it's hard to come back to Oklahoma sometimes, because of my li'ili'i self.

Do you see anger as having a positive value?

Anger is anger and there's going to be anger where there are human beings. Everything has two sides to it and more uses than two. We've all experienced the negative aspects of anger; we're here. There's a Gandhi quote I never get quite right about anger, anger is what he used to transform his country. It became a useful power. I try the "standing on the moon rule," which means, stand on the moon and look down at your problem, your country, your family, your heartache, your failure. Then it all makes sense. Practicing the arts is a means to transform or transmute anger into something useful.

What you said this morning about war triggered my question. You were saying "there's a war in me and I have been able to claim that, take responsibility for that, separate myself from it, even while condemning it."

Yeah, it was difficult to recognize that War was in me. I have more than a fair share of pride. When I began to really examine this war within myself I then found a common link between myself and those I name my enemy. Maybe being born with the blood of two warring tribes within has come to some good use. Or I'm just fooling myself. The most difficult thing is to allow the contradictions to exist, side by side. One always wants to swallow the other.

Last night you said most poetry is not in a book. I want to hear more about that.

Books are a relatively recent invention in human time. The roots of poetry are oral; most poetry comes about with a guitar, a drum, or some sort of accompaniment, announces itself in the world with dance. I am not a good researcher or scholar, but I imagine if you were to go back and look at the roots of all cultures in the world, most of the poetry that has been produced is probably born in song. Many songs are languishing and lonely for people to remember them and speak them. It's possible to call some of these forgotten ones back. I consider poetry as song language, as soul talk . . . .

From that, how do you define poetry?
Song language.

And "soul talk"?
Soul talk, song language. That's only one definition. There are as many ways to poetry as there are to God. Say that to your poetry fundamentalist!

Your wisdom voice is so communicable and clear without simplifying things. The poem "When The World As We Knew It Ended" is power-ful, haunting, and sometimes I've had tears in my eyes when I've read it; I feel you were singing about anger having the possibility for trans-forming. Maybe you were coming to the kitchen table to find what you needed to release, and maybe you wondered as Americans, you and me and all of us, or as humans, what it is we need to come to the table to release. I don't know if it's a question or just a place to go into.
That was one poem that practically wrote itself . . . . I don't think I was coming to release anything in that poem. The kitchen table is at the heart of the human world. It is also a metaphorical device. Meta-phor implies surprising link, a generative relationship. I had no idea what was going to happen once I stood there in the poetic field, the poetic house.

What do we need to release to each other in the world we find our-selves in?
There's probably nothing better than to be able to sit down with peo-ple you care about, or friendly strangers when you're exhausted and lonely and far away from home, sit across the table and eat with each other and visit and laugh. I remember going to my cousin George Coser's the last time I was in Oklahoma. He's always very sharing, very giving, and he knows the old stories, the ones that few people remember. Our last visit we talked about how those visits were our university seminars, our colleges. I used to drive my elderly aunt Lois

Harjo around Creek country to visit her relatives, friends, and the old ones who still knew the stories. Genealogy is a web of stories about people, the tribe, and our combined journey from a mythical real past into the present. Within this web are retellings of historical events, philosophy, astronomy, origins of meaning, medicine; it's all there. But he was bemoaning that we don't have time anymore. Our communities have been blown apart by loneliness. No one knows who they are anymore, or where they belong.

How much time do we look at that little hourglass on the screen?
The computer is useful, and the Internet world is a genuine storytelling space. It is yet another experience of time and place. Nothing replaces the direct experience of story or song. Many stories and songs carry life-giving forces in them. They have certain purposes. E-mail language tends to be much more curt or short. Text messaging is communication in its barest form. There's no face, no history, just an ever-present now in which we are too busy to craft a reply, no place for subtlety, history, or connection.

An assignment might to have students write an essay, and then to have a student say the same thing in an e-mail, to translate, from one rhetorical context to another.
Yeah, that would be a good one. And what happens in between.

I want to ask you about myth and talk about the importance of myth: myth as sacred truth and something that human beings need and yearn for. How does myth get transformed into pernicious ideologies? I think of the horrible things that have been done because people have used myths to defend the myth of ourselves as God's chosen people who are bringing enlightenment to the savages, and conquest and imperialism and genocide and all kinds of terrible things done because people are connected to a myth in a kind of pernicious or poisonous or destructive way.
I guess we need another word then, because my translation of myth is root stories, or rather, the shifting, dynamic template of spirit from which a people or peoples emerge. It is not some imagined past, rather, the dream works of the communal self.

That just wouldn't be a myth or . . . story?

I hear what you're saying . . . Cotton Mather stands at the beginning of the "mythic" creation of American in his drab Puritan cloak, foaming with righteousness. Hence, Native peoples are evil. Who does this serve? An economy in which those on the side of God are the winners and keep all of the money? I'm heading back to the moon to take another look. My sense of the mythic is a root that's larger than each small cultural group. We're all eventually related. When you look from the moon, we all look the same.

I guess one of the inevitable questions when you come here and it is the state centennial, what different voices do you hear within you? Do you hear different voices, that polarity, that Oklahoma state centennial celebration?

Again, I climb back on the moon. Many of us with Oklahoma roots have dreaded the upcoming celebration of the Sooner State centennial. I can understand the state wanting to celebrate its incorporation, but not everyone in the state has cause to celebrate. The state represents land theft and second-class citizenship for many of us. The state came about over land theft, broken promises, and in the wake of Cotton Mather's hatefulness, which is repeated in Bible belt fundamentalism. The Oklahoma state motto "The Sooner State" honors those who jumped the line for first dibs on land claims. They were the quicker thieves. Statehood is about gun power, and the ability to takeover and control, as much as it is about gathering together a community. At the center of Mvskoke philosophy is a term: *vnoketcv*, which is, compassion. You look for the best in any situation, and keep moving about with grace, no matter the trial. We were uprooted from our homelands and moved to Indian Territory, were promised to be left alone. Then oil was discovered on our allotted lands. Now there are genetic patents sought and secured on our plants, our medicines. Still, we're dealing with gun power. So it seems to me that to celebrate the centennial means that we celebrating a takeover. The best possible outcome is perhaps a conversation between the citizens of Oklahoma. Has this come about from the centennial? One day there will be that conversation. Everybody will sit down at the table: Cotton Mather and his people, my people, the eagle, the stone, the plants, the winds, all of us. And we will be equal. And everyone's voice will have a place.

Or "you have to learn English."
The English Only laws are preposterous. There's Cotton Mather again. English is not the Native or only language of this country, or of Oklahoma, either.

It's interesting that you're from here and the two states you live in, New Mexico and Hawai'i, are more known for indigenous populations.
They're the only two states in the United States with a non-European majority.

And you just gravitated.
New Mexico, I went there for Indian school. It's been home to me; to my art. Oklahoma is also an origin place for me. It's where I was born, where I was raised until I escaped to Indian school, to New Mexico. When I return I always return to a force field of contradiction, of love and hate. And yet over the years I return for family, tribal responsibilities, for the beauty, and to hammer and work it out . . . and here we are at this table, so we all have a place at the table But that's part of what I was given: the test, the puzzle. For me, Oklahoma is one of those challenges, and one of many gifts.

And for me Hawai'i is a place of refuge and inspiration. I continue to learn from the water, and I also learn from the hula tradition. The stereotype of hula does not even touch the reality of this epic tradition. It's an oral, poetic tradition that includes dance, genealogy, the ocean, astronomy. At my ceremonial grounds there's a story that links us with Hawaiian. Sam Proctor tells of seven canoes coming up from Polynesia to the place we lived, before Oklahoma or Alabama and Georgia. We are since related. That's something you won't find in books; although I've been reading of archeological discoveries in the last few years that back it up. So there's a Hawaiian-Mvskoke connection. It makes a poetic leap of sense.

You have talked about Toni Morrison and Emily Dickinson as writers who had a significant impact on you, and I was thinking, like with

Toni Morrison, I can remember reading her for the first time and feeling like I was reading English, but it kind of wasn't English, and part of what she had had to do was create a new language. As a reader I had to transform myself to be able to read the language, and that was what was so wonderful and exciting about it. I was wondering if you think of yourself as changing the language through the poetry you do, or creating a new language.

I like the way you put that. Toni Morrison did create her own world of English. She made a space in novel form that would allow her and her people and their stories, and her telling of them to live. Her stories have rejuvenated American literature . . . world literature. All artists like to think their work will help rejuvenate culture, and art.

Most people just carry forward what they've learned without adding their own spirit. As a child in elementary school in Tulsa, I loved drawing and was constantly making art of some sort or the other. In kindergarten one afternoon, I intently worked on my drawing, a colorful design with people linked in a circle. It wasn't anything I'd ever seen before. The idea just came to me. Then I took a break, looked up, and noticed that everyone was drawing the same square house with two windows, the same lollipop tree. I asked the group: "Why are you copying each other?" They looked at me like I was crazy, then started copying me. That stayed with me. To repeat the norm was to make a secure place. Some of us grow our art vertically as we create directly from classic traditions. Others work more horizontal and gather together from many other traditions and places.

This interview transcribed by Diana Silver and Ted Stoller.

John McBride is a geologist and avid reader who has followed his dream and opened what is becoming the finest bakery in Oklahoma City: Prairie Thunder.

Elaine Smokewood is a professor of English at Oklahoma City University, and served as chair of the English Department for six years. She is also a published poet and a teacher of poetry.

Harbour Winn is a professor of English and film studies at Oklahoma City University. He is the director of the Center for Interpersonal Studies through Film & Literature, as well as the OCU Film Institute. He directs the annual April poetry series.

The Craft of Soul Talk

[Interview with Susan Thornton Hobby, summer 2009]

You once said that the first piece of poetry you recognized as poetry was a jazz riff on the radio. Could you talk about that recognition, and about poetry's relation to music for you?
A jazz riff became a ladder into the middle of the heart of sound. I traveled from room to room in the heart of the horn player. This was while I was acquiring language. I was aware that most of my comprehension of adult conversation was basic. I was communing and understanding at a level that was quite complex, a level beyond words, beyond current time or three-dimensional vision. The music gave me the means. It was poetry. I believe most children have an awareness they bring with them to this realm. Words were more daunting. I was insecure with words. I began speaking late, and maybe because of this I was very aware of the power of words. Around the time I was transformed by listening deep to the jazz riff, my father threw me across the room. I had repeated an expletive my father often used, in front of his friends. That was visceral power. I took note. Still, I came to love words, especially as they were sung. I leaned toward repeated phrases and the sing-song rhyming of nursery rhymes, and the heightened language of lyrics, and in the poetry of Emily Dickinson, whose poems always struck me, because they made their own, distinct sound sense.

You were a painter, a dancer in your youth. How did you start to write poetry?
The first poem I remember writing was unmemorable. In eighth grade Mrs. Costello told us to pull out our paper and pens and write a poem. We were baffled. What? Poems? She gave no other instructions. She

wanted to have material to submit for a statewide anthology of student writing. She submitted my poem, and a story I wrote earlier in the class. The story got honorable mention. The poem disappeared. At Indian school I wrote songs for an all-Indian acid rock band. They also disappeared. And I also wrote some poetry, mostly as notes passed between us in classes taught by Bureau of Indian Affairs employees who had given up teaching long ago. (Though some of the teachers were inspired and their efforts were life-changing for us.) Mostly the poems rhymed and some were limericks commenting on our various dramas. On the side I was reading Thomas Hardy poems and novels. It wasn't until I was a pre-med student at the University of New Mexico and met Simon Ortiz that I began trying poetry again. Or rather, I found myself in love with poetry again, after listening to Simon, Leslie Silko, and Leo Romero. The revolutionary times in Indian country demanded that my spirit learn to sing with words.

At your reading, when asked about the Iowa Writer's Workshop experience, you laughed and said, "I survived." Could you explain?
I honor my Iowa Writer's Workshop experience; however, it was challenging. My poetry mind had come up through a nonacademic focus, even though my final undergraduate major was in creative writing at the University of New Mexico. Poetry for me was soul talk, crafted soul talk. Words literally had power to change the weather, to make things happen. Poetry was a way to document the spirit of a people. I didn't quite fit in and found myself lost in the workshops. Craft is essential to all art, even soul talk. The teaching emphasis on craft and critique appeared to intellectually gut the process of poetry. Yet even as I floundered and failed in that system, I found my own direction. I was close to Sandra Cisneros, Dennis Mathis, and Jayne Anne Phillips, who all studied with me there. And I befriended a guest teacher, Rosalyn Drexler. All have remained important to me.

Your book She Had Some Horses, *written in 1984, is being reissued by Norton. What do you think it is about this group of poems that speaks so powerfully to people?*
I often ask myself that, because I see all the flaws. I asked the Pomo/Miwok novelist, tribal chairman Greg Sarris, about this during a frus-

trating time. My best poems aren't in that collection. He said it was because the book made a cohesive story, of sorts, and it was teachable. And I have to acknowledge that the book came into being because some ancient horses approached me. They are in the book. They had momentum and taught me. That's part of the book's power, I think. The horses' unspeakable power, charged the poems and gave them impetus.

Could you speak about your ancestor, Monahwee, and specifically, about his relation to animals?
Monahwee knew how to bend time. He could speak with horses and was known as a fine hunter. He also knew medicine. His mind and knowing were in an age of a different construction of consciousness. When you invest your mind to knowing energy in science you give yourself over to experts. When you understand the world as a world of consciousnesses, including animal consciousnesses, then you are a participant.

Animals are throughout your poems—wolves, eagles, panthers, crows, not to mention horses—what do they help you say?
Maybe it's the opposite!

You write about reciprocity—of giving back to the earth, of balance. Sounds like something that is missing from our world.
My focus lately has been the study of energy. Everything is energy. A poem is an energetic matrix given shape and meaning by words, phrases, silences, voice . . . it is a giving back, to dreams, to relationships, to the spirit of an age. If we understand that there is a kind of consciousness in all creations, both natural and human-made, then we are constantly in a state of reciprocity, though often it's unconscious. Gratitude ups the spin of consciousness. It gives consciousness. Ignore and it will fall away unacknowledged.

You've talked about a silence that was killing you, and that writing helped ease that pain. Does writing give something back to you?
Always.

Susan Thornton Hobby has written for newspapers and magazines for more than twenty-five years. She is a contributing editor at the *Little Patuxent Review*, and a consultant for the Howard County Poetry and Literature Society. She lives and works in Maryland.

INTERVIEWS

"Our Star." © Joy Harjo

"We Will Go Together." © Joy Harjo

"Towards Portland." © Joy Harjo

"And There You Are on the Other Side." © Joy Harjo

ii

Columns
by Joy Harjo

Global Roots

[*Muscogee Nation News*, October 2006]

Last week I went for a walk along the ditch here in northwest Albuquerque. It was bare. It had been shaved of the mile-high weeds and flowers lining it throughout the summer. There was a lull in the water flow so the bottom was now only mud and occasional pools of water. In a few spots crayfish were looking for soft muck. Green heads of frogs emerged here and there. Some frogs took the opportunity to sunbathe. They dove in alarm at the sound of humans or dogs. One wise frog was not so skittish. He sat out on a concrete abutment, taking in the day. I sat with him for a while to see what I could learn. Frogs are rare these days; poisons and pesticides have taken many out. This wise frog and his relatives were the most I'd seen in one place in years. Neither of us said anything as we watched the blue fall sky sweep by, and the scrambling crayfish. At the back of my mind was the stack of papers on my desk, the errands, terrorist attacks by our government, and concern for my brother and his heart. The tightness of fast society slowly unwound. When the wise frog did finally talk he noted that humans used to come and visit. And they would visit in turn. We both sat with remembering as another stream of blue passed with thoughts of clouds. We felt sad at the current state of loss in this world of progress. Somewhere along the way humans got confused and lost the way. Some still remember, I told the frog. I look for those who remember everywhere I travel. He nodded. Some of his people had forgotten too. Time pulled us both apart. We had to get on with it. We made plans to get together again. We thanked each other for the visit. When I looked back he was still there, encouraging that crayfish towards a muddy cove.

In the news this month was a story about scientists who are looking for a cure for gay sheep, or rams. They are experimenting with giving the rams extra high doses of estrogen to see if that will counter the tendency for their own kind. Sounds funny to me: the scientists, not the rams. This study probably cost more than a block of new homes for the elderly. Why not come up with a cure for hatred or judgment? We'd all get along a lot better if we'd respect each other. The wise ones don't judge people by the color of their skin, by accumulation of wealth, or by inborn traits. It's how we treat each other (human, frog, etc), and how we take care of our many gifts, that matters. I wonder what Mekko Frog would say about this? He's probably laughing about those poor rams prancing about on high doses of estrogen, in the name of science.

In the latest *World Literature Today*, published in Norman, Oklahoma, the cellist Yo-Yo Ma said something in an interview with Michelle Johnson when talking about the Silk Road that sparked me thinking about growth of our Mvskoke culture:

"Years ago in Japan, a wise man told me that if you look deeply enough at anything thought of as local—be it music, an idea, a tradition, a craft—you find that the local thing has global roots. We think of ancient people as being so isolated, yet here is this trade route along which religions and music and musical instruments and foods and goods all traveled. Of course, people traveled with them, and the people and the goods and the ideas and everything else all had enormous influence on one another."

I think of the Mississippi River, the Gulf coast, the Atlantic, and the Caribbean, as part of the network of Muscogee trade routes. Now these routes have been expanded by air flight. I consider what has come to be known as Muscogee culture. Our culture contains many threads leading all over the world. Every day when I practice my sax I say a *mvto* to Adolfe Sax. He was born in Belgium, spent most of his life in Paris where he gave himself over to promoting his family of saxophones. He was vilified and booed by jealous competitors for inventing the saxophone. The sax eventually made it across the Atlantic, found a place in jazz and American music. It's one of the favorite instruments of Creek people. Jim Pepper is still the reigning jazz sax king. I remember Thomas Berryhill. I'd love to hear of others. Even my paternal grandmother Naomi Harjo played sax in Indian Territory. One of these days it might be considered a Mvskoke traditional instrument. That's how these things happen. You never know.

Identity

[*Muscogee Nation News*, December 2006]

Hensci. We've finally landed in winter after a long summer and fall. Here on the Rio Grande flyway geese and cranes have been passing over. Only thing is they aren't always headed in the right direction. I've watched several layered vees of birds head south, then turn back north. Others fly east or west in a confused manner. Strange. I never saw this growing up in Oklahoma. In the fall, birds flew south. In the spring; they returned. Since the hard freeze of the last few weeks they are definitely and quickly flying south. No question. At least the Sun still comes up from the East and sees us through until nightfall, and returns again. A *mvto*, or thank you for the Sun.

We just survived Thanksgiving. Most people don't know that it's a holiday based on a fabricated story of a sit-down dinner with Pilgrims (a mispronunciation of the word "pillager") and Indians. The Pilgrims weren't too friendly, were rather grim, not the sort to hang out and eat with Indians. The holiday was an invention fostered by the writer of the poem "Mary Had a Little Lamb," Sarah Josepha Hale. Maybe the poem should have been, "Mary Had a Little Turkey." Did her family own a turkey farm? Of course, most of us enjoy any kind of excuse for a day off, for eating lots of good food with family and friends, and for some (not me) an afternoon of football games. I take issue with the compromised premise, and with all of those people dressing up as fake Indians. For most of the world, turkey feathers in the hair and buckskin, equals Indian.

Once, years back in a class I was teaching, we studied images of Indians. One of the students took sheets of paper and markers to a preschool class in Boulder. She asked the children to draw an Indian.

They all drew one of two images: a warrior on horseback brandishing bloody tomahawks, or delicate princesses, most of them on horseback. They weren't human beings, rather symbols, and the children had already internalized them.

When my daughter was three, just before she went into Head Start, we went to sign her up at a preschool in Iowa City (where I was going to graduate school). The children surrounded us and danced around doing that Hollywood war whoop, you know the one. Their teacher was embarrassed. I was amazed that children that young had already taken in that false image that had nothing to do with being Indian, or Mvskoke, or Acoma, my daughter's other tribal affiliation.

We're still mostly portrayed in those flat images in art, literature, movies, and not just by non-Indians or three-year-olds. The worst culprits are often our own people. Of course, we do have warriors on horseback, and I saw a little tomahawk brandishing in my early days, and most of our princesses aren't so delicate. They like to eat.

A few years ago I carried a fussy grandson, accompanied by his older sister, for a stroll around the Santa Fe plaza, while their parents (and the rest of the diners) finished dinner in peace. Desiray, who is Mvskoke, Acoma, Navajo, and most decidedly "Indian looking," paused in front of a Plains headdress displayed in an Indian jewelry shop for tourists. "Look Nana," she said. "Indians."

Identity is a complex question. How do we see and define ourselves and how do others define us? What do governments have to say about it and what does the wisdom beyond the foolishness of small-minded humans have to say about it? I understand there are many in the tribe who believe the tribal membership should be made up of only fullbloods. Yet many of these same people sing hymns and espouse a religion that isn't Mvskoke in origin. There's a contradiction here. I have no issue with people talking with or worshipping God in whatever manner or form. Diversity in form describes the natural world. What I take issue with is the rigidity and hurtfulness of such an exclusionary vision. Such a plan to limit tribal membership is not only racist, it's genocidal. It's what the makers of the Dawes Act had in mind in the first place, like a sustained-release genocide pill. And many have bought into it. Self-righteousness stinks, no matter how it's dressed.

Behind this are some real issues and concerns about what it means to be a real Mvskoke person, about our responsibilities, and about having some say in the shape of the future of our nation. Race figures greatly into how one moves about the present world. A fearful approach doesn't work, in governments, societies, or our individual lives. We bring about what we fear as surely as we bring about what we love. Both carry the same charge. Let's try some common sense and compassion. I've talked to many of our tribal members in Oklahoma and elsewhere in the country who have expressed concern that their children and grandchildren are being denied a place in the family, our Mvskoke Nation. Is this who we want to be, a people who throw their children away? If we look with the mind of the vastness and complexity of the viewpoint of the stars, then we will see and know wisely.

Finally, a few closing words from poet Louis Littlecoon Oliver, who always had a wise word or two, and a sense of humor. He was a full-blood, born of Koweta Town, Raccoon Clan. In his book, *The Horned Snake*, he says: "I asked the oldest of my old ones what his opinions were of the white man's supertechnology: his flight to the moon, his atomic weapons, his present status in the Middle East. He stared into the fire for a moment, then looked up at me with a faint smile and said: 'We look upon the white man's world of wonders as trivia—and short-lived.' "

Censorship and the Power of Images

[*Muscogee Nation News*, May 2007]

This last month has truly been a time of coming and going. I traveled across the Atlantic to Stuttgart, Germany, for the *Indianer Inuit: Das Nordamerika Filmfestival*. The film festival featured videos and movies from all over Indian country, from full-length features to short documentaries. Tantoo Cardinal, a well-known actress from Canada, appeared in several of the films. She was at the festival to introduce one of her films, *Unnatural and Accidental*, based on a true story of a series of deaths of Indian women on Vancouver's east side in the 1980s due to alcohol poisoning. The deaths weren't taken seriously because the women lived on skid row, until a common acquaintance was found. He had killed them by pouring alcohol down their throats. The images still disturb me. Did the retelling of the story bring about a healing? Can testimony bring peace? Or did it unnecessarily recreate the destruction?

Years ago I was hired by the White Mountain Apache Tribe in Arizona to write a one-hour drama that would incorporate the healing story of the *Gaan*, the mountain spirit dancers. I was taken in and told the story and the meaning of the story. There are as many versions as storytellers, though the core elements are the same. I witnessed a beautiful ceremony in which the *Gaan* appeared from the mountains and danced. In the screenplay the protagonist (lead character) was a teenage Apache boy at Indian school in Phoenix. He got caught up in a gang, began drinking, and started getting into trouble. The family brought him home. A ceremony was done for him. He literally and metaphorically became a part of the story; as he healed he became the boy who was the central character in the traditional story. And as in the traditional story, the *Gaan* appeared to teach the people in a time when they had forgotten their origins, a time when strange crimes were being committed, a time of unusual weather and natural disasters, when the people had forgotten to take care of each other.

(These times sound awfully familiar, don't they?)

Each draft of the screenplay went to the tribal cultural board. One of the older women objected to a scene that depicted drinking and fighting. The images were disturbing, and thus the images had power to cause disturbance to the viewer. This was not something we need to see, she said. We need positive images for our people. The next meeting she had changed her mind. Her granddaughter read the script and convinced her that the drinking and fighting scene provided an important part of the story, though it was difficult to watch. The scene might help others in trouble see themselves, could act as a warning, and present the challenge faced by the young man. We included a scaled back version of the scene in the final screenplay. (I hear the video is still very popular there, and is copied and passed around the community.)

Since then I have carefully considered the power of images and how they affect us. I used to be a huge fan of all the various *CSI* and *Law and Order* shows. The stories are dramatic, well written, and each hinges around the solving of a crime. I began to notice that in almost all in the shows the crimes were perpetrated against beautiful young women and children. And the crimes became more and more heinous and creative as the season went on (just as the crimes we see and hear reported in the newspaper, television, and the Internet these days). The brutal images were haunting and were beginning to instill a fear, a distrust of life in me. I checked every corner and closet in my house before sleeping. I worried about the safety of my family. When I stopped for sleep, those terrible images would play about my mind. I quit watching.

Ratings go up commensurate with sensationalistic images, which usually involve fast sex, violence, and drugs. And with ratings come sponsors who will pay more for their commercials, advertisements for food that isn't really food, for more goofy or violent TV shows, happy drugs, or a myriad of clothes, cars, and gadgets that we don't really need. And we get hooked, because nothing is required from us but our complacent, exhausted minds, which are complacent and exhausted because we're eating the food that isn't really food, watching stupid shows, taking all those happy drugs, and working eight or more hours a day to buy all those things dancing across the television screen. This, I guess, is what they always meant by civilization, or progress.

Still I am opposed to censorship. If you don't like these images, or the turn the story is taking, then turn off the television, make your own stories (even for television!), pull out your paints, your poems, get to work on those ribbon dresses you promised two years ago for your nieces, cook your own dinner and take some to your neighbor. Start visiting each other again. And take the kids with you. You'd be surprised at the gifts we are carrying in this nation. Share them.

Images of Indians, most of them not created by us, have defined us in the world. Germany has a great fascination with Indians. To understand this obsession you have to know about Karl May, a German writer who at the turn of the last century wrote a series of extremely popular Wild West stories inspired by the a stilted, stereotypical novel *The Last of the Mohicans* by James Fenimore Cooper. Winnetou, whose adventures are captured in the stories, makes his appearance in the first chapter with these words: "His bronze-coloured face bore the imprint of special nobility." May vividly imagined fantasy Indians and the Wild West. He never met a real Indian. I guess everyone wanted and still wants that "imprint of special nobility." Now there are over 200 Indian clubs in Germany. In these clubs people make authentic costumes, take on Indian names, dress up, dance, and live as Indians for the weekend.

Once during a visit to Griefswald, a city on the North Sea, near Poland, I was taken to an "Indian Museum." The first floor was framed images from American magazines and books. The second floor was displays of exquisite, perfect Plains Indian beadwork made by Germans. This is why a real Native man who looks Plains Indian, has long hair, wears lots of leather with fringes, a few feathers, and can take a stoic pose, can make a living being Indian in Germany, by making appearances and sharing "culture." Run that by the next high-school career day in Okmulgee. We do need ambassadors who can show that real Indians are all kinds of Indians: long, short, funny, sad, male, female, child, old man, skinny, fat, human being . . . some of us dress up for powwow, some of us dress down for life.

After the last film the organizers, who were some of the most thoughtful and organized organizers I've met on my travels, closed with a ceremony of thank-yous and acknowledgments. At the end, an elderly German gentleman whom many of us had noticed on the front row of all the screenings jumped up and enthusiastically asked: "What about a thank-you for the audience"? We all smiled and clapped. Later over dinner I heard his story. The old man came to all the *Indianer* film festivals because when he was in the war, a Lakota man, who was part of the U.S. forces, captured him. That Lakota man really looked after him and he was convinced that's why he was still alive. He carried around an image of an Indian as a kind soldier.

It's the small kindnesses that will be remembered.

It's Difficult Enough to Be Human

[*Muscogee Nation News*, June 2007]

It's dusk of yet another day. It wasn't an easy day, yet it was a blessed day. There were mangos from the mango tree, the sun came out to visit and give life, and the earth once again supported us and gave us beauty and a place to live. I did not have to leave my refuge here on the side of the Koʻolau range overlooking Honolulu. No flight to catch, no insecure security, no possible TB-carrying passengers coughing in my direction. And this house was surrounded by singers: all kinds of birds, clouds, plants, and insects, each with their songs (most of them love songs, just like humans), and they overruled the neighbor's noise. Her hearing is bad so she pumps up her music and television, which is everything from popular Hawaiian hits to Japanese pop to Korean soap opera. She often plays the same song over and over and over. We can hear everything up here on this slope. I've heard fights and breakups, love trysts (cats seem to be getting the most action in the neighborhood), family celebrations, and once a mother tending a sick child who coughed through the night.

It's all here, and in a sense everywhere is here. We're in the same story wherever we are, though the details might be different. I've even heard my children cry from heartbreak, though I have been a thousand miles away in physical distance, even as I have felt their joys. I'm convinced that the birth cord transcends time and distance, and that women are anchors and bearers of knowledge in a profound way, a way that scientists have not gotten around to study because most of their knowledge is pertinent only to the male body, and their knowledge is rooted in three-dimensional linear thinking. Most medical research is based on the male physiology. Most knee implants, for instance, are designed and manufactured for the male body, not the female.

I also think about how most of what we read or hear is through a European-male voice or point of view. Even when we go back and look over what we know to be Mvskoke history and story, as it appears in books or other accounts, nearly everything is filtered through this voice and point of view, and those who have been educated have learned to see through that lens. The first visitors skewed our story, or should I say, skewered? Our particular Native female and male experience has no place here.

Years ago when I was in my fervent twenties I stood with Leslie Silko, the Laguna Pueblo novelist, outside her Tucson home while she tenderly watered a garden she had fortressed against predators. That morning I asked her why her protagonists, or main characters, were mostly male. Tayo in her novel *Ceremony* was male, as were many of the characters in her short stories. Leslie responded thoughtfully. She has never been one short on words, yet her response stays with me all of these years: "because males are more vulnerable."

That our men are more vulnerable made sense to me, especially our Native men. It's difficult enough to be human, and hard being Indian within a world in which you are viewed either as history, entertainment, or victims. Our males are as sensitive as the women, and carry gifts forward that have difficulty finding a place in a world that does not honor them. It's not an impossible test, but it wears away at the spirit. "Our men" is often a major topic of discussion among women. We must bear up with them, support them, and stand firm when they fail and want to take us down with them, yet continue to help raise them up. Without our brothers, fathers, uncles, grandfathers, we are people without a rudder. Men are under immense pressure in this system to disrespect their mothers, sisters, aunts, and to disregard the gifts of women and female power. We need both male and female power to create anything in this realm. We need both the Sun and the Moon. We are earth and water, just as we are fire and breath. We are each evidence of male and female power, all the way back to the very beginning. I remember when growing up in Oklahoma that the worst thing one boy could call another was a "girl" or a "woman." And why is that? To disrespect women you disrespect your mother, your own source of life.

I was told a story by a friend who was at a gathering at a Maori *marai*, which is a community/spiritual house, sort of like the ceremonial grounds square and the mound complex combined. A young Maori man had gone out into the world, graduated from the university, had a high-paying job and a new car. He came back home full of ideas and ripe with his own sense of power and prestige. (They aren't always the same thing.) During a discussion an older woman stood up to speak. He admonished her and told her women were not allowed to speak. They had no power in this place. She rose up anyway, and lifted up her skirt. "Have you forgotten where you came from?" she demanded. She spoke. When she spoke, she addressed him as son.

We continue to be imagined by those who know nothing about us, or imagine us as quintessential Plains warriors in the Wild West shows. And worse yet, we start believing that's who we are, that tradition means wearing and becoming these constructed images.

I didn't watch *Bury My Heart at Wounded Knee* on HBO last week. I knew I would be disappointed, even angry. Hollywood can't seem to get past the Cavalry rushing in to kill everybody. Hanay Geiogamah did watch the show and though he has been part of Hollywood productions for years has realized the brutality of Hollywood. In a response he says:

A feature article on the making of *Bury My Heart* titled "The Last Stand" in the May 27 *Los Angeles Times* gives a brief, perplexing account of how Hollywood came to the view that American Indians can now be justly and fairly seen as co-agents of their own destruction. As a two-hour condensation of the book, "The film didn't have time to dwell on the spiritual, Earth-friendly image of Native Americans," says the article's author, Graham Fuller. "Nor does it offer a politically correct perspective," he adds. The Sioux, we're told, were "as rapacious as their white conquerors."

This view is scaldingly laid out with the portrayal of Sitting Bull as a baby killer, as a coward who hid in his tipi at the height of the Battle of Little Bighorn, and as a greedy buffoon who lusts for the white man's money and approval.

The scriptwriter, Daniel Giat, confidently tells the *Times*, "My primary objective was to fully dimensionalize these people. Sitting Bull was vain. He was desperate to hold on to the esteem of his people and win the esteem of the whites. But I think in depicting his desperation and the measures he took in acting on it, it makes it all the more sad and tragic, and I think we identify with him all the more for it."

To complete this grim, determined view, the film presents every Indian cliché imaginable in graphic, full-bodied images without context or explanation: brutal scalpings; stoic, saddened faces of Indian elders; sick, dying babies; herds of wild horses surging across open prairies; vast armies of Indian warriors mounted along high vistas; war ponies being ceremonially painted; desperate ghost dancers, and heartless Indian agents and schoolteachers. We've seen them all far too many times.

Hanay goes on urge us to get out of Hollywood and get back home and work from our own communities. Hollywood will never get the story right.

This means we are going to have to get our own story right, and take charge of the direction in which we are headed. What kind of story are we making? Is it one in which the junk-food corporations win and we all die of diabetes and other "food"-related illnesses? Is it one of name-calling and pulling each other down? Or is it a story of facing the challenges together, each of us? Are we telling the story in our own voices?

A cascade of military transport planes heads over my house on the way to kill in Iraq. In the predominant story coming from the country's leadership, "we" are killing for peace, for democracy. It doesn't work that way, for words without roots in honesty and respect can and will do things recklessly. Iraq is the new Indian country. The corporations want oil. Sound familiar?

Maybe if we take care of our own story of our people, and make a story of justice, honesty, with a vision of caring for all within the tribe, we might inspire the same in others. If I remember the story correctly, we had no need for jails, for institutions, for military transport jets. We had everything we needed. We took care of each other.

What a story.

Excerpt from Hanay Geiogamah, "End of the Hollywood Trail: Bury My Heart at Wounded Knee," *News from Indian Country,* online at http://indiancountrynews.net.

Dehumanization Flatlines

[*Muscogee Nation News*, August 2007]

Every time I fly south I return with another piece of our collective Mvskoke story, another memory. In Peru a few years ago I was in the *fekce* of the western hemisphere, the place of many indigenous roots. Last week, after Green Corn, I flew from Tulsa to Medellin, Colombia, in South America. Most of us here know of Colombia because of coffee, and Medellin because it was the battleground of the cocaine drug trafficking cartels. I have learned a different Medellin. I saw immense crowds of people come out to hear poetry. They love poetry as much as sports. They appreciated the whole spectrum of poetry as it was presented by the more than seventy poets from all over the world. The poetry didn't have to be hip-hop or over the top to catch attention. There were oral poets, classical poets, eyes-on-the-page poets, poets in Spanish, English, and many other languages, including at least eight indigenous languages. (They got to hear a little Mvskoke). The same kind of audience you would have found at the Creek Nation Festival. Even the children sat in rapt attention and listened. The last night's performance was in an amphitheater that held several thousand people. The seats overflowed and people sat out on the hills, for poetry. The performance went almost five hours. The highlight for me was the reading of the indigenous poets. We performed together: Hugo Jamijoy of the Putamayo Nation; Fredy Chicangara of the Yanacona Nation; Lindantonella Solano of the Wyuu; Jessie Kleeman, Greenlander Kalaait Inuit; Natalia Toledo, Zapoteca; Gregorio Gomez, Guarani Nation from Paraguay; Allison Hedge Coke, Cherokee; Sherwin Bitsui, Dineh; and me.

What I value most was the small moments of time we had together.

It's these small memories that make up the bulk of the content of all poetry, of our lives. We ate three meals a day together in the Gran Hotel and performed in various combinations with the other poets all over the city. We talked about family, about friends in common, joked, shared histories, talked about the extermination policies of governments, about worldwide earth changes, and about what is always, and remains eternal. We compared stories.

Lindantonella's people have been targeted for extinction by the paramilitaries. Right now in the northern part of Colombia, her homelands, the people are being massacred. The multinational corporations have discovered riches beneath the earth and are laying claim to oil, gas, and other minerals. And this is going on in nearly all the tribal nations in the South. Sounds horribly familiar, doesn't it?

Allison reported that she, Sherwin, and Fredy saw a very poor native woman sitting on the sidewalk with an infant, not far from the hotel. The mother was feeding her baby orange soda in a bottle. It was all she had. Allison went to buy food and milk. When she approached the woman to give her the bag of groceries, the mother panicked. She grabbed her baby and ran. Fredy interceded and told her that Allison just wanted to give her food. She took the bag, said "bueno, ciao," then disappeared in the street. Fredy said that there is a market for stolen children, especially for people in the North. She thought Allison had come to steal her baby.

For Fredy's people coca is a beloved plant. It is good for circulation, for the blood. His people's relationship with coca is similar to our relationship with ginseng or *heles hvtke*. Coca leaves carry the prime ingredient in the manufacture of cocaine. And cocaine in its refined state is highly addicting and surrounds itself with guns, greed, and violence. The manufacturing process dehumanizes coca.

The beloved corn, of our people (and the people of the South) has also suffered dehumanization and is now, in its refined state, contributing to the diabetes epidemic. Corn processed as corn syrup appears in a very high percentage of refined foods. We become addicted to it. The essence and the meaning of corn and our relationship to it gets lost and perverted in the process. Consider tobacco and how it has served us traditionally. It too has been dehumanized by process, by lack of respect in its use.

How much have we been dehumanized by the manufacturing pro-
cess of a consumer culture that does not value our essence as a people?
And what happens to any of us in a dehumanized state? Massacres,
bureaucracies, racism, cultural-ism are all outcomes of dehumaniza-
tion. We learn to do it to ourselves and learn to dehumanize each
other. In the process we lose respect for ourselves, and for those plants
and elements that have accompanied us since the beginning. We also
lose poetry.

My understanding is that we have three minds, yet they make one
continuum. One takes care of everyday details, is linear; it's the orga-
nizer. It takes information directly from the five senses. The second is
the gut-heart mind, or *fekce*. It's the mind of memory, the carrier of the
ancestral knowledge. It is the knowing mind. The third is the intuitive,
the beyond-human-knowing mind. It doesn't know time and space.
It is beyond time and space. It is the compassionate mind. All things
make sense here.

Dehumanization flatlines us to think and be in one dimension, or
one mind. Think about it: most of our education in these times, and
most of our presence is in the linear "buy-now" mind. Even language.
Metaphor cannot happen in the linear. I've heard the Mvskoke- and
Hawaiian-language people speak about how we're losing metaphor,
the ability to address several levels of meaning at once in our expres-
sions. Our old language is full of potent sayings. Language ripples
with meaning.

Always something to consider . . . and I appreciate those who have
carried forth the poetry of our ways. There we were in the middle of
the sky of that summer night, dancing with the fire. Or as Natalia
Toledo says in her poem "Origin": "We were a flake of God, / flower,
deer and monkey. / We were the torch that split the flash of lightning /
and the dream told by our ancestors . . . "

Mvto.

"Origin" by Natalia Toledo from *Prometeo*, nos. 77–78, July 2007, Sixteenth International Poetry
Festival of Medellin.

We Are Story Gatherers

[*Muscogee Nation News*, June 2008]

We are story gatherers. That's what we humans do. The bird people and others who move about are up to the same thing. Ever watch a dog gathering stories from bushes, posts, or the back end of another dog? Same thing! She or he is literally picking up messages about who's been there, who they were with, what they were eating, where they were going . . . sound familiar? We always have our ears open for the best stories. Note that the stories we remember aren't of the ones who sit back, do nothing, and point fingers and talk. Anyone can do that . . . . And each of us is in the midst of making a story, our own story. And as we make our own story we're carrying forth the story of our family, our clan, our tribal people, and a larger time and space, so large we cannot comprehend it.

One story I keep turning over and over in my mind is how a friend of mine from up North, Candyce Childers, was healed. She was very ill, an illness that was scraping loose the bottom of her soul from her physical body. One night, the Mother Mary appeared to her, and healed her. Candyce was grateful for the healing but mystified at the appearance of Mary. She did not attend to the Catholic belief system in which she had been raised. Her mother, a Catholic faithful Athabascan woman, told her it was her mother's prayers to Mary that had basically set up the resonance, the connection. Her mother, Candyce's mother told her, had loved Mary and prayed and spoke to her constantly. Consider that those prayers had literally set up a bank of assistance for her descendants.

When I write these columns I always feel the presence of Henry Marsey Harjo, my great-grandfather. He loved to gather inspirational stories and share them. I am in the stream of his thinking, his love. I have felt other relatives and helpers around for other occasions. We all continue to help each other.

This past Memorial Day I was terrified as I got ready to take part in an around-the-island paddle in honor of my canoe club's 100th-year anniversary in Hawai'i. I'd been up the night before running through all kinds of "worst thing that could happen" scenarios. I had never done what is called a "water change." This meant having to either leap off the canoe into deep ocean and climb onto the escort boat, or take the escort boat out, follow the canoe, then when it's time to make the change, leaping off the escort boat into the ocean, swim to the canoe and climb in, while continuing to paddle. My spirit wanted to do it. My will was wavering.

Then, there I was, standing on the edge of the escort boat; about to leap into the choppy waves of the deep blue, and the approaching canoe I had to swim to looked much farther away than I imagined. I looked out and was surprised by a tremendous love for the ocean. I felt my father's love for the water. I jumped.

In retrospect, I believe that the leap was healing for me, and more than that, it will remain as a foothold for my grandchildren, something they can use when they must make a leap to get to the next higher place within themselves. And then . . . there's the story.

We Are the Earth

[*Muscogee Nation News*, August 2009]

What a summer, and it's not over yet. It will go down as the summer Michael Jackson died, the summer of high unemployment and a shifting economic system. It will go down as one of the hottest. The heat is what's on everyone's mind. I knew Oklahoma was going to be hot as I made my way there with a vanload of grandchildren for Green Corn. It was hot in New Mexico when we started the journey, and even hotter in Oklahoma. I bought an outdoor thermometer and took it to the ceremonial grounds to see exactly how hot the temperature ran. In the sun, the temperature read 120 degrees! In the shade it dropped to 112. Tonight, a few weeks later, I listened to the news of record low temperatures in the Midwest. These high and low running temperatures are Earth's fever and chills. We are Earth. We're in an unstable condition. We are headed for some rough ecological times.

It's not every summer we make it back for Green Corn. Last year I couldn't afford the plane fare. This year I returned to New Mexico, and because the journey is over land, I can drive. Early Friday morning after arriving, two of my granddaughters and I headed over to the grounds to set up. The oldest is Haleigh, just turned sixteen years old. She listens deep, beyond the frequency of chatter. Desiray Kierra is a fresh and fierce thirteen-year-old. There's so much to tell them, so much they need to know as they begin their journey as women in a world of immense changes.

We left from my sister's house in Glenpool and took the back route. This meant turning off the Beeline east at the Beggs exit, then taking a road south, some miles on the other side of Beggs. I trust that I will once again recognize the turn and the zigzag out to the ceremonial grounds.

Several turtles crossed the road. I angled to make sure one who was in the path passed safely beneath the van. We braked for a butterfly. Within a few miles we veered into the opposite lane past the body of a coyote who had been hit by a car. Buzzards fearless with hunger lifted when we passed, then they quickly landed and continued their feast. "They're doing their job," I told my granddaughters. "We all have our tasks in this world. These days, we humans have been more trouble than help with our trash and amusements."

I told them to make note of signs. We can forecast with clouds, shapes, by watching the animals and how they are moving about the earth. We began looking for the road south. I don't recall the name of the road because I know it when I see it. Yet, as we continued driving west the landscape began looking unfamiliar. We were surprised when a bird dove close and glanced off the front of the car, and relieved when it flew away unhurt. Then immediately ahead of us, to the right, we saw a crow surrounded by three sparrows. They berated and dove at the crow. I pointed this out to the girls and I turned the van around. Within a few miles I saw the road south we'd missed. The usual landmark of building and signs had been razed and the corner was now a flat field.

We continued toward the ceremonial grounds on that old road that goes from great grandparents, to grandparents to mother, daughter and to granddaughters, with our ribbon dance dresses, cooking and camping utensils piled up in the back. "This is where we come from," I told them, "and where we are going. If you pay attention to the signs, you will always find the way."

A Way to Speak Their Souls

[*Muscogee Nation News*, February 2010]

This morning I'm in Anchorage, Alaska, and at 7:15 a.m., it's dark as night and will be until close to 9 a.m. I was invited up for the first Native Playwrights Festival at the Alaska Native Heritage Center. The playwrights are from Native villages around Alaska, and from here in Anchorage, Fairbanks, and Juneau. Some of us performed on Saturday, and the workweek began Saturday evening with meetings. We've been meeting every day from 8:30 to 5. Then we have work assignments at night. So I'm scrambling to get my column in (as usual!).

I first came up to Alaska in the early eighties to go to the jails and prisons and help prisoners with poetry. Rent-A-Wreck was the only car rental company that would rent without a credit card. And guess what kind of car they loaned me . . . a refurbished police car! It was just what I needed to drive up and gain confidence of the prisoners! I went to four different penal institutions in the Anchorage area, *four*, with a population half the size of Tulsa. One was a women's prison. About 90 percent of the prisoners in the men's units were Native. Black men were next in population size, then the poor white guys who'd come up to work on the pipeline. Most were in primarily for being Native, black and/or poor with no money for attorneys, and/or doing something stupid in the wrong place at the wrong time. I did not pick up malevolence, but neither was I placed in high security. I met the brother of a friend of mine, who is now a shaman. He'd been riding around with a party and got picked up. The women were mostly in for taking the rap for their boyfriends, and being in the wrong place at the wrong time.

I'll never forget being led into a room of male prisoners by the jail keep at the Fourth Avenue jail, and hearing him say "I'll be back in two hours" as he locked the door shut behind me. The prisoners were hungry to speak and sing. Most of them knew poems by heart. There were tears and laughter as they wrote and spoke. All of them responded to poetry because they needed a way to hear and speak their souls. They took to writing with a hungry fervor. I'm convinced that most waywardness is creativity turned backwards.

There's a young moose who has been roaming the grounds of the Alaska Native Heritage Center. Tourists who don't know moose think they're cute with the personality of deer. They are more dangerous than bears. Bears are predictable. Moose will charge, kick, and then dance on you, and not think about it. One woman's cousin just had her scalp pulled loose by a dancing moose. So we had to navigate the young one as we walked out to use the Inupiak village site for a classroom. (There are several kinds of traditional houses in the on-site village.)

My brother has been having a hard time getting his citizenship card. He used to have one. He was turned away because our father's name had "Jr." on one document, and not on the other. All the rest of us in the family have our cards. Even his son has his enrollment card. My brother needs the card for health care. He's been having stroke tremors. But the receptionist kept telling me: "He's not in our system." We were here before there was a system. We have been Creek for thousands of years, before cards. I know my brother isn't the only one who's been having a problem. I'm afraid he might not live long enough to get his card.

And finally, don't forget, be kind to all you meet along the way.

Energy of the Transaction

[*Muscogee Nation News*, April 2010]

It is supposed to be spring. It's trying to be spring. I wake up this morning to freezing temperatures, and it's almost April in New Mexico. I remember Oklahoma springs in childhood. I felt like a small plant and knew myself as part of the earth. I'd get up before anyone else. I liked the smell of the medicine of plants, and felt the snakes, earthworms, horned toads sliding and walking about, including the mole who lived in the yard moving through the earth. In those times, robins came only in the spring. Our backyard was full of poison ivy. We had to be careful, especially our sister. She was highly allergic to it. Mostly it didn't bother me. The front was carpeted in clover patches and dandelions. I knew these plants intimately and practically lived in them in the spring and summer. I knew June bugs, roly-poly bugs, and played with them.

I liked getting up when the sun got up. The breaking of dawn was my time to just be, without the worry or pressure of any family drama. I liked being with thoughts that were fed by the sun, by the trees, plants and the creatures. I usually had a dog. They always followed me home. When I was five, I had a dog I named "Alligator." I've always had a fondness for alligators, some kind of connection I don't totally understand. It isn't my clan. My clan through my father is Katcv, or Tiger clan. I don't know my mother's Cherokee clan, even though her mother was raised Cherokee near Moody, Oklahoma.

I knew the bees and played with them as freely as I played with the garter snakes, horned toads, and the other creatures. I'd play house. I'd catch the bees, hold them in my hands, and set them where I wanted them. They didn't mind me handling them as long as they could get on with their business. They had a tender mind toward me as a young one.

One day I was out playing in the late morning. My mother and her friends were sitting out on the porch, drinking iced tea, smoking cigarettes, and telling stories. Usually the stories ran along the lines of who came home and who didn't come home, and all the drama going on among them and their families. My mother was also writing songs at that time. She was still at home and didn't have to work yet. Her best friend was another Cherokee woman who lived across the street. I liked hearing them talk, their presence there. I adored my mother. She was beautiful, dynamic, and loved to sing.

As they talked I continued my play in the clover. I caught bees as I often did and played with them. My mother and her friend saw me. I can still see my mother's concerned expression and hear her alarmed voice, "You'll get stung!" It was then the bee stung me. I felt betrayed and confused by the situation. I didn't pick up bees again for years.

Watching the World Shift

[*Muscogee Nation News*, July 2010]

This morning a class of university students visited me from the University of North Carolina Pembroke, led by professors Jane Halliday and Jesse Peters, along with the Isleta Pueblo novelist and Institute of American Indians Arts professor Evelina Lucero. The class is traveling about and visiting Native writers in the Southwest.

We visited over breakfast at Flying Star, and then they came over to my place. I showed them the painting by my grandmother Naomi Harjo, of the Seminole/Creek leader Osceola, who was my great-uncle by way of my grandfather Sam Checote. She signed with her name, and the year 1916. We talked of Osceola and his story and how much he continues to inspire as we continue to challenge the story of America. The talk turned toward the massive oil spill in the Gulf waters. Someone in the class pointed out that oil is blood. Oil is gushing out into the ocean and destroying ocean, earth, and the plants and animals who depend upon clean waters and fertile earth. It is a raw and widening wound. This disaster is so emblematic of the history of the colonizers and the disregard for the life spirit of the natural world. For many, many years oil has been greedily sucked from the earth, with no regard for the spirit of the oil and of the earth, and for the universal law that states we take only what we need. We are not to be greedy. And we are to give back. Oil continues to gush in the thousands and millions of gallons into the beloved waters. Gary Farmer, the Mohawk actor, musician, and cultural entrepreneur, had told the class the previous morning that so many of these out-of-control natural disasters are happening because the indigenous people who protected the places were moved or killed and aren't there to take care of them.

In 1990 I was present at a gathering of indigenous peoples from all over the Americas, to discuss where we were as indigenous nations in light of the upcoming hemisphere-wide celebrations of Columbus to take place in 1992. We were meeting up in the mountains at a tribal village just outside Quito, Ecuador. I'll never forget the arrival of the people from the Amazon villages. They walked up to the encampment barefoot, with their beautiful, colorful feathers and spears. They came to share a story of American oil companies, and how the lands were being destroyed and their way of life irrevocably broken, as their lands were rich with oil. They came to ask for help.

I keep thinking of the how the wound opened in the Gulf is connected to the initial landing of the explorers who would set off mass destruction of peoples, cultures, and resources. It began in the same waters as the spew of oil. Like most of us, I keep watching development of the story on television and on the Internet. Yesterday I watched a man carrying a dolphin in his arms to try and help him. The dolphin was sick from oil contamination. The dolphin died. Now turtles are headed through the slick to lay eggs. Many turtles are being burned by oil fires. I have heard that some of the workers have committed suicide after helping with the cleanup because to see such destruction hurt their spirits. This unnatural natural disaster will have consequences that many cannot even imagine.

My mind always goes back to the prophecies of our own visionary Phillip Deere and others like him. They warned us for many, many years of these earth changes and advised us to change our behavior, but we did not take heed. It is crucial that we don't give up in our minds and hearts as we watch our world shift. As the visionary Deere and others have predicted, the world will be looking towards Native people for answers. Will we be ready?

"The End of the Season." © Joy Harjo

"Turtle Portrait at the Ceremonial Grounds." © Joy Harjo

"We Give Light." © Joy Harjo

"Between the Sky and Earth on the Way to Chicago." © Joy Harjo

iii

The Last Word

Prose Pieces by Joy Harjo

Preface for *She Had Some Horses*

[From the second edition, W.W. Norton, 2009]

"What do the horses mean?" is the question I've been asked most since the first publication of the book *She Had Some Horses* in 1984. I usually say, "It's not the poet's work to reduce the poem from poetry to logical sense." Or, "It's not about what the poem means, it's 'how' the poem means." Then I ask, "So what do the horses mean to you?"

Like most poets, I don't really know what my poems or the stuff of my poetry means *exactly*. That's not the point. It never was the point. I am aware of stepping into a force field or dream field of language, of sound. Each journey is different, just as the ocean or the sky is never the same from one day to another. I am engaged by the music, by the deep. And I go until the poem and I find each other. Sometimes I go by horseback.

No, that's not it at all.

The horses are horses. My father's side of the family is inextricably linked with horses. We aren't a Plains horse culture, though we came to know horses. I understand there was some exchange of power between the horse people and my relatives from seven generations or more back. I am the seventh generation from Monahwee (sometimes spelled as "Menawa"), who is still a beloved person to the Mvskoke people. I was told how he had a way with horses. He could speak with them. And he also knew how to bend time. He could leave for a destination by horseback at the same time as his cohorts, then arrive at his destination long before it was physically possible to arrive. He had a little black dog that followed him everywhere.

My cousin Donna Jo Harjo was a champion barrel racer and knew how to speak with horses. She had to live close to horses or not live at all. They were her people as much as any of the rest of us.

And there was the horse that came to see me once in the middle of a long drive north from Las Cruces, New Mexico, to Albuquerque. I perceived him first by an ancient and familiar smell. Then I was broken open by memory when he nudged me, in that space that is always round and through us, a space not defined or bound by linear time or perception. He brought the spirit of the collection of poems that was to become *She Had Some Horses*.

Later was my horse Casey. The last time I ever drank too much was in a "proletariat bar" in Krakow, Poland, because I was happy to meet and play music with some Bolivian Indian musicians and a Hawaiian, and we were all so far from home. In the gray of the early morning, when I was whirling around sick in my hotel room, my horse Casey came to me with a worried look. He was concerned because his last "owner" had died of complications from alcoholism. I assured him that this would not happen between us. And it didn't.

Horses, like the rest of us, can transform and be transformed. A horse could be a streak of sunrise, a body of sand, a moment of ecstasy. A horse could be all of this at the same time. Or a horse might be nothing at all but the imagination of the wind. Or a herd of horses galloping from one song to the next could become a book of poetry.

I follow in the tracks of gratitude. I thank the horses, my ancestors who loved them, and those who grew to love their cars and trucks instead. I thank my mother and her family. They are the ones who brought me songwriting, guitar players, and singing. I thank Simon Ortiz for singing original and old horse songs. I thank the shaman/healer I saw perform a poem and become what he was singing. It was then I began to comprehend the true power of the word: the dangers, the beauty, and all the healing elements. This was when I began to write poetry. I thank those who continue to believe in the horses, in poetry.

What a journey.

The Art of Resistance

[Preface for *Indigenous People's Journal of Law, Culture and Resistance*, 2004]

Resistance:
"the act, on the part of persons, resisting, opposing, or withstanding
Or, simple refusal to comply with some demand, without active opposition,
Or, the power or capacity of resisting."
—from *The Compact Edition of the Oxford English Dictionary*

As a means to power, as in resistance providing the impetus for conductivity of electricity.

As when my uncle, the Seminole/Creek leader Osceola, who when asked to sign a treaty that would have moved his people from their swamplands in the Southeast to lands west of the Mississippi, plunged his knife into the treaty paper. This was highly symbolic, and yet it wasn't solely metaphorical. His people, our people, never surrendered.

Or a meeting in 1990 of indigenous peoples of the hemisphere, from the Arctic Circle to Tierra del Fuego, in Ecuador to consider how we move respectfully from the common experience of colonization into the next span of creation. Amazon tribal people showed up barefoot with stories of oil companies spoiling the water, the land. People from Guatemala were fearful of retribution for even attending such an event. They could pay with their lives or the lives of their relatives.

Or the Western Shoshone Dann sisters who continue the charge to take care of their lands in Nevada, though the United States wants the land for a bombing range. They have been harassed and threatened by federal agents, have had police convoys and livestock trucks impound their tribe's cattle tended to by the Danns, and once a six-day raid ended with 269 horses captured and killed. Their lands have never been ceded or deeded to the U.S. government.

Or calling into question a recent development in Playa del Rey that will unearth the graves of the indigenous peoples of Catalina Island.

To the smaller and most powerful acts, including speaking your Native language to your children though you are awash in a sea of English.

Or planting corn of different varieties though it's easy to buy perfect corn from the supermarket.

Or rising at dawn every morning and greeting the sun as a relative, and continuing to remember gratitude along the way.

Or finding a way to step through shame though you have been beaten or raped or repeatedly told that you are inferior because you do not fit neatly into the mold of civilization because you are too dark, too light, too much, not enough, too poor, too backwards, and you have stumbled into an alcohol or drug blur to dull the pain, and you stand up.

Or finding a way to love ourselves, though we fight, we cannot come to agreement, and are stubborn and jealous peoples.

There are countless acts of resistance concurrent with numerous heroic stands for justice throughout the hemisphere and the world, as usurper governments, organizations, companies, and churches fought and fight for control and ownership of indigenous lands and resources. This journal being born into print is an act of resistance against silencing and supports the charge for viable, healthy communities. The need to protect one's inalienable right to life (as human beings, and as a community-nation of beings) is basic. We are charged with life when we breathe and are embraced into this world. That breath seals our promise to walk with integrity into this earthly place. It is that simple.

We are born into dynamic systems. They are bound together by language, woven with complex layering of myth, stories, and songs. A dynamic system sends out new shoots, flowers, collects harvest, rests to recollect meaning; then the process starts all over again. If a system is stymied, smothered or swallowed up, it lies fallow, adapts, or dies. But, no matter what happens, that original plant, animal, human, or culture does not become the interloper, no matter what the interloper does. The plant, animal, human, or culture might be influenced by the interloper, and the interloper in turn influenced by that which it is trying to destroy. No matter, both will be changed in the interaction.

This is the crux of the matter. We resist because we are exactly who we are, and no amount of warring, genocide, propaganda in the name of education, or preaching will turn us into anyone other than who we are. We are as beautiful and terrible as any other soul or nation. We have a right to develop and grow. We will change, because change is sure and inevitable; it's how each system in the world grows into deeper knowledge of itself. We have something to offer, though our knowledge may counter the desires of interloper nations.

What especially makes indigenous cultures unique is the relationship to the land. Land is a being, an entity, a repository of meaning. There is an ongoing relationship between human beings and the land. It is the keeper of our bones, stories, and songs. In this manner of thinking/being there is no hierarchy to differentiate value between all living things. When we say "resistance" it often means we are resisting a way of thinking about the land and each other. We do not consider the land something to be bought, sold, or cultivated "Resistance" means honoring this relationship, means honoring this life force, and those powers of this earth that feed and inspire us. The Euro-Christian version of progress then doesn't represent progress at all. It has come to represent greediness, lack of respect for otherness, and the need to swallow up and destroy anything different than itself. Civilization doesn't appear to have resulted in progress at all in terms of an evolution of kindness, of overall quality of life.

There is an art as to how we resist. Osceola's act was dramatically symbolic. It was also an act of desperation by a human being who had seen his aunts, uncles, relatives dragged from their homes, children forced from parents, his friends killed in front of him, because some people wanted their lands for themselves. God had promised them. To be seen as equal human beings with souls is still at the root of the continuing need for resistance. We resist being treated disrespectfully.

We resist by continuing to stand up with integrity for what is right for all. We also resist by writing, singing, making new art, reviving and continuing older classic traditions, by rewriting law, making new law, even by collecting our papers, poems, stories, and art into an indigenous law journal.

Perhaps most of all, we are resisting being imagined out of existence. I return to Osceola standing there at that moment in history. It is a terribly dynamic moment for though we have changed, we are standing there still.

Afterword for
The Delicacy and Strength of Lace

[From the second edition, Graywolf Press, 2009]

This correspondence between Leslie Marmon Silko and James Wright in the late seventies remains a classic in epistolary literature. Like finely crafted lace kept as a story of beauty and struggle and passed between generations, these letters possess a liquid and elegant power. We admire the knit of soul. We recognize the struggle to be artists in the midst of the daily challenges of living.

Many of us who were becoming poets in those times turned to Wright for the beautifully crafted humanity of his poetry. His immense compassion for what is American: the up and down of history, horses, and the seasons of forgetting and remembering drew us to the grasses, plains, and rivers of his expression. He was a teacher, a poetry ancestor for my generation. For those of us of struggling to create from diverse traditions in literature, Silko led the way as she brilliantly merged traditional indigenous storytelling and song language with European/American forms of written story and poetry. Silko's visionary poetic storytelling crossed over and made a recognizable and fresh American literature. Each story has a soul and a time and place in which it is rooted. She made a template for many of us to raise up our own creations.

Though an artistic legacy may be immense, each is constructed of everyday intimacies as they play out within the ceremony of sunrise and sunset, of night sky and morning light. There's the ornery rooster, the rainstorm climbing over a mountain and revealing a rainbow on a grey day in Italy, children, illnesses, and the many births and deaths of consciousness. This correspondence between Silko and Wright frames such legacy.

How we gather stories, songs, and poems and share them has changed since the writing and publication of these letters. Few write such missives these days. Most letters are notes quickly typed on keyboards as e-mails or by finger on cell phones as text mails. Time has speeded up. We don't have time anymore, to be human. Gathering stories, making stories and sharing them in a dynamic back and forth defines our humanity. "We used to go visit and stay for days, sharing stories and songs with each other," my cousin George Coser, Jr. told me last time I was home and visited him for several hours. These letters are such communication on paper. Yes, things change.

And yet, what stays the same is the searching for beautiful and wild sense in the world. Essentially, the publication of these letters passes them on to the next generation. Maybe there will be a forthcoming book of e-mail communication, or even text messages between artists who struggle in the midst of making the story of their lives. However it happens, and it will, we walk either knowingly or unknowingly in the path of our literary ancestors. We hold their legacy like exquisitely crafted lace in our hands.

In Honor of Patricia Grace

[*World Literature Today*, May–June 2009]

A beautiful day has been loaned to us. Your arrival makes it great.
Oketv semvnvckosen pom pvlhoyes. Momen pom vlakeckat heretos.

From far you have come and we say thank you. Your great work we value.
Hopiyen vlvkeckat mvto cekices. Cem vtotketv vcake tomekv, ecerakkueces.

You honor us and we honor you.
Ceme porakkuececkat, matvpomen ece rakkueces.

We have lots of love/respect for you.
Vnokeckv sulken cemoces.

E te rangatira, tena koe. Nga mihi aroha. Ka nui te aroha kei waenganui i a tatou.

This means, "Greetings to you, esteemed leader. Greetings of love.
There is much love between us all [gathered here]."

We were all created by a story. Each and every one of us, walked,
swam, flew, crawled, or otherwise emerged from the story. It is terrible
and magnificent being, this story. Each of us has a part. Each thought,
dream, word, and action of every one of us continues to feed the story.
We have to tend the story to encourage it. It will in turn take care of
us as we spiral through the sky.

Every once in a while a storyteller emerges who brings forth pro-
vocative, compassionate, and beautiful tales, the exact story-food the
people need to carry them through tough transformative times. Patri-
cia Grace of the Maori people is one of these storytellers given to the
people of Aotearoa, and now to the world as she is honored as the
twentieth laureate of the Neustadt International Prize for Literature.

What distinguishes Grace's storytelling in the novel, short story, and children's book form is her ability to reach back to the ancestors and the oldest knowledge and to pull it forward and weave it together with forward-seeing vision, to create what is needed to bring the living story forward. She uses the tools of grace, humor, humbleness, and wisdom to make the design. The design is not extravagant or show-off; it is exactly cut and crafted to fit the shape of Maori culture and ideals. In Patricia Grace's stories everyone has a voice. In her stories, there is no separation between the land, the water, the sky, and the will of the people. Those relationships are honored.

If we have gathered the materials to make a structure with rapt attention and songs, and have followed a protocol of respect, then as we construct the story it will want to come and fill that place; it will endure and inspire. And we will endure and be inspired. Grace's stories make a shining and enduring place formed of the brilliant weave of Maori oral storytelling and contained within the shape of contemporary Western forms. We are welcomed in and when we get up to leave, we have been well fed, we have made friends and family, and we are bound to understanding and knowledge of each other. We become each other in the moment of the story. We understand that we have all been colonized, challenged by the immense story we struggle within. We are attempting to reconstruct ourselves with the broken parts. Patricia Grace's stories lead us back towards wholeness, to a renewal of integrity. This is the power of story. This is the power of Patricia Grace's gift to the Maori people, to indigenous people and the world.

Last year as I prepared to present Patricia Grace's legacy to an esteemed panel of jurors from all over the world I called together an informal meeting of Pacific Islander writers in Hawai'i. We sat at a table in Manoa, over home-cooked food and refreshing drinks. I had researched everything I could through books and the Internet and wanted to know what Grace's own people, what other writers from the Pacific had to say about her and her writing. I heard many things that afternoon. I was told of her extensive help in mentoring young writers, that she writes from within a Maori community, she always went beyond as she published a substantial and continual solid body of literature and raised her seven children. . . . We talked about how there's a Maori level and an English literal level and how each story contains a storehouse of wisdom and knowing. . . . "It's about time an indigenous person finds their way into these kinds of circle" said one. "She's an ambassador for Maori women." Her novel *Cousins* restores women to the story of history. "Her range of Maori voices is unparalleled . . . she has exposed the Maori world to the rest of the world, showing that Maori people are as diverse as any other." All the stories at the table as we talked about Patricia Grace kept spiraling back to respect, love, and accomplishment in these times of immense difficulty in our indigenous communities.

Finally, as I got up to leave, everyone wished me well in the presentation, but agreed that with such competition from world-known writers, Grace wouldn't have much of a chance. "We know her and love her in the Pacific," they said. "She's one of our treasures. She isn't known far outside the Pacific. At least the jurors will come to read her and her work might find a way through them." We now know the ending to this story and we are here to celebrate. I must acknowledge the panel of jurors who were enthusiastically supportive of Grace. I did not have to do much convincing at all.

Joining me in celebration here tonight with their words are a few of Grace's Maori colleagues.

Kia ora taatou.

I send my greetings and my family's *aroha* to Patricia Grace for her Neustadt laureateship. The distinguished jury chose eminently well. Patricia Grace has mentored and encouraged many younger writers through her work with the Maori writers' organization, Te Ha (which means the breath), and through the example she has set being an ambassador for Maori writing and culture internationally. I have always looked up to her with admiration for this generosity, given all that she has achieved in literature. Her children's books have represented to New Zealand children all their wonderful possibilities from a Maori perspective, and have become classics in our nation's literature. Her novels similarly engage Maori artistic potential, and bring us to the same literary table as New Zealand's most successful women writers, Janet Frame and Katherine Mansfield, and all of our brothers and sisters who are renowned for their literary prowess from our Pacific region, and elsewhere. Patricia is our first Neustadt laureate, and also the first Maori woman to publish a

literary collection. I thank you for choosing so wisely this author who is of our country's community of writers, and of her tribal people. She is a national *taonga*, that is, highly prized by those who respect great writing. Patricia is our *rangatira*, our leader. She is an important compassionate voice, an immensely patient and nuanced voice, who shares Maori values and thus furthers our community. *Arohanui* to you, Patricia. Your writing brings *Mauri Ora*, the well-being of life's energy, to us all.
—Robert Sullivan, poet (Nga Puhi, Ngati Raukawa, Kai Tahu, Galway Irish)

Pat's work is such an inspiration to all indigenous people, to indigenous women, and especially, to Maori. We are very proud of her and gratified to see her honored by this very distinguished organization for her considerable contribution to the world of literature. Without writers such as Patricia Grace the world would know little, or nothing, of the enormous struggle Maori and other indigenous people all over the world have had, and continue to have, to survive, and hopefully, to thrive. Patricia Grace gives us a voice, she tells our stories, she shows in very human and personal ways the damaging effects of colonization and how we continue to exist and to prosper in spite of those. Her stories remind us that we are connected, to our past from which we draw wisdom and courage, and to others in similar situations around the world. As a Maori woman and a teacher of literature I am especially grateful that Patricia Grace continues to write us into the wider world picture, adding our experiences to those of human beings everywhere.
—Reina Whaitiri

Mvto, mvto, Patricia Grace, for taking care of your gift and sharing with us.

I Used to Think a Poem Could Become a Flower

[Introduction to *Ploughshares*, December 2004]

I used to think a poem could become a flower, a bear, or a house for a ravaged spirit. I used to think I understood what it meant to write a poem, and understood the impetus to write, and even knew a little something of the immensity of the source of poetry. I was never the scholar and approached the study of poetry like a fool in love with the moon. I mean, I am a reader of poetry and know a little something about the various indigenous roots of American poetry. I know even more about European elements of verse, because it was what we were taught in public schools, hammered as the "truly civilized poetry." I had to stand quite a distance from the earth, beyond conquest politics, to see the foolishness of this assertion. To say one form of poetry ranks above all others is to insist on a hierarchy of value that arbitrarily rules that a rose has more value than an orchid because it is a rose.

It was in song that I first found poetry, or it found me, alone at the breaking of dawn under the huge elm sheltering my childhood house, within range of the radio, of my mother's voice. I used to think that the elm, too, was poetry, as it expressed the seasonal shifts and rooted us. Ever since, I have given myself over to poetry. Poetry, like the earth, was once decreed flat, then round. I declare it as a spiral in sha~ ' movement. Each strand of poetry curls from classical form a~ unruly forms that often overtake and become classical ' tendrils of songs coil into the future.

I used to think a story would house a beginni~ and could be contained within the covers of a ⊦ in the heart. Or that a story in any of its ~

away from myself, show me a world so different I would return to gaze at my known universe with a newly shining mind. I believed that myth was alive and was the mothering source of stories, poetry, and songs, and within this field I would find the provocative answers to the riddle of being a human without wings or gills, or directions to a map for a lost wanderer. I was looking for vision, for the powerful and startling and subtle strategies of language, pattern, style, character, and voice that would satisfy and, even more, inspire. I have given myself over to the making of stories, and even as I found them or they located me, I was ecstatic, and then bereft. For then there I was again at the same place I started, the beginning of a page or a voice. I garnered hope, but hope is wistful and empty and is like water in our hands.

I confess. At this moment in the time and context of being a writer in America, I don't know whether I believe or know anything that I once thought I believed or knew about our art of truth-telling, of singing, of constructing the next world as a story or series of stories that we will eventually inhabit, as will our children and their children. Maybe we've all been through this before, but it's another version and we're in it deep. I used to imagine writing as a ladder leading us from the blind world into the knowing world, but now to imagine a ladder means to imagine a land or a house on which to secure a ladder. For many of us in these lands now called America, imagining this place has been a tricky feat, because there is no place that hasn't been or won't get stolen, polluted, or destroyed, and for all of us now planted here, the foundation is shaky, because though it is strong with vision, the country was founded on violent theft. But this is what we have, who we are here, together. And we can use the fire still burning there to destroy this place, or build it anew with bricks made of the trash, with fresh, shining inspiration. The elm is still growing there in that yard.

Maybe the ultimate purpose of literature is to humble us to our knees, to that know-nothing place. Maybe we here on this planet are a story gone awry, with the Great Storyteller frantically trying out different endings. Whatever the outcome, we need new songs, new stories, to accompany us wherever we are, wherever we go. That's the power contained in a book, journal, or magazine that you can carry in your hands. So, these stories, poems, and songs are offered as such, as for challenge, for inspiration, for sustenance.

THE LAST WORD

Talking with the Sun

[From *This I Believe*, July 2007]

I believe in the sun. In the tangle of human failures of fear, greed, and forgetfulness, the sun gives me clarity. When explorers first encountered my people, they called us heathens, sun worshippers. They didn't understand that the sun is a relative and illuminates our path on this earth.

Many of us continue ceremonies that ensure a connection with the sun. After dancing all night in a circle we realize that we are a part of a larger sense of stars and planets dancing with us overhead. When the sun rises at the apex of the ceremony, we are renewed. There is no mistaking this connection, though Wal-Mart might be just down the road. Humans are vulnerable and rely on the kindnesses of the earth and the sun; we exist together in a sacred field of meaning.

A few weeks ago I visited some friends at a pueblo for a feast day celebration. The runners were up at dawn and completed a ceremonial race that ensures that the sun will continue to return. It is a humble and necessary act of respect. And because the celebration continues, the sun, the earth, and these humans are still together in a harmonious relationship.

Our earth is shifting. We can all see it. I hear from my Inuit and Yupik relatives up north that everything has changed. It's so hot; there is not enough winter. Animals are confused. Ice is melting.

The quantum physicists have it right; they are beginning to think like Indians: Everything is connected dynamically at an intimate level. When you remember this, then the current wobble of the earth makes sense. How much more oil can be drained without replacement, without reciprocity?

One day, recently I walked out of a hotel room just off Times Square at dawn to find the sun. It was the fourth morning since the birth of my fourth granddaughter. This was the morning I was to introduce her to the sun, as a relative, as one of us. It was still dark, overcast as I walked through Times Square. I stood beneath a twenty-first-century totem pole of symbols of multinational corporations, made of flash and neon.

The sun rose up over the city, but I couldn't see it amidst the rain. Though I was not at home, bundling up the baby to carry her outside, I carried this newborn girl within the cradleboard of my heart. I held her up and presented her to the sun, so she would be recognized as a relative, so that she won't forget this connection, this promise, so that we all remember the sacredness of life.

"I Can See You from the Mango Tree." © Joy Harjo

About the Authors

Joy Harjo was born in Tulsa, Oklahoma, and is a member of the Mvskoke Nation. Her seven books of poetry, which include such well-known titles as *How We Became Human: New and Selected Poems*, *The Woman Who Fell from the Sky*, and *She Had Some Horses*, have garnered many awards. These include the New Mexico Governor's Award for Excellence in the Arts; the Lifetime Achievement Award from the Native Writers Circle of the Americas; and the William Carlos Williams Award from the Poetry Society of America. Harjo's most recent publication, *For a Girl Becoming*, a coming-of-age book for young adults, appeared in 2009.

She has released four award-winning CDs of original music and won a 2009 Native American Music Award (NAMMY) for Best Female Artist of the Year for *Winding through the Milky Way*. Her most recent CD release is a traditional flute album: *Red Dreams, a Trail beyond Tears*. She performs nationally and internationally with her band, the Arrow Dynamics. She also performs her one-woman show, *Wings of Night Sky, Wings of Morning Light*, which premiered at the Wells Fargo Theater in Los Angeles in 2009; recent performances have occurred at the Public Theater in New York City and the La Jolla Playhouse as part of the Native Voices at the Autry.

She has received a Rasmuson U.S. Artists Fellowship and is a founding board member of the Native Arts and Cultures Foundation. Harjo writes a column, "Comings and Goings," for her tribal newspaper, the *Muscogee Nation News*. She lives in Albuquerque, New Mexico.

Tanaya Winder is a poet, spoken-word artist, and musician from the Southern Ute and Duckwater Shoshone Nations. She is a nominee for the First Peoples Fund's Jennifer Easton Community Spirit Award and a recipient of the 2009 Lynn Reyer Award in Tribal Community Development. Winder was a finalist in the 2009 Joy Harjo Poetry Competition and a winner of the A Room of Her Own Foundation's spring 2010 Orlando Prize in poetry. Her work appears in *Cutthroat Magazine*, *Yellow Medicine Review*, and *Adobe Walls*.